About the
EDITORS

Chris Sinacola has more than 35 years of experience in journalism, marketing, health care, and freelance writing. He was a reporter and editor at the *Worcester Telegram & Gazette* from 1987 until 2015. He is the author of *Images of America: Sutton* (2004) and *Images of America: Millbury* (2013) and editor of Pioneer Institute's *The Fight for the Best Charter Public Schools in the Nation* (2018) and *A Vision of Hope: Catholic Schooling in Massachusetts* (2021). Sinacola holds a bachelor's degree in Italian Studies from Wesleyan University.

David J. Ferreira spent his professional career as a vocational-technical teacher, coordinator, and principal, 16 years as superintendent of a regional school district, and was inducted into the Diman Regional Voc-Tech Hall of Fame. As Executive Director of the Massachusetts Association of Vocational Administrators, he advocated for high-quality programming for voc-tech districts and collaborated with postsecondary institutions and apprenticeship programs. Mr. Ferreira received his master's degree in Secondary School Administration from Providence College. He served on the New England Association of Schools and Colleges (NEASC) Commission on Technical and Career Institutions and the state's Vocational Technical Advisory Council and was an adjunct faculty member at the University of Massachusetts Boston, and Fitchburg State University.

Hands-On
ACHIEVEMENT

Massachusetts's National Model
Vocational-Technical Schools

EDITED BY **Chris Sinacola & David J. Ferreira**

PIONEER INSTITUTE
PUBLIC POLICY RESEARCH

PIONEER INSTITUTE
PUBLIC POLICY RESEARCH

Pioneer's **mission** is vto develop and communicate dynamic ideas that advance prosperity and a vibrant civic life in Massachusetts and beyond.

Pioneer's **vision of success** is a state and nation where our people can prosper and our society thrive because we enjoy world-class options in education, health care, transportation, and economic opportunity, and where our government is limited, accountable, and transparent.

Pioneer **values** an America where our citizenry is well-educated and willing to test our beliefs based on facts and the free exchange of ideas, and committed to liberty, personal responsibility, and free enterprise.

CONTENTS

A Hands-on Approach to Closing the Knowledge Gap

by Thomas F. Birmingham and William F. Weld

"It is not by muscle, speed, or physical dexterity that great things are achieved, but by reflection, force of character, and judgment." –Marcus Tullius Cicero, *De Senectute*

For years, many in the Commonwealth's educational and economic development communities have lamented the existence of a "skills gap," alleging a sharp disconnect between the skills high school and college graduates possess and those that employers need. As Massachusetts's information-based economy grows ever more complex—in high technology, computers, health care, education, life sciences, and other fields—the need for highly trained and highly flexible workers has become critical to our economic future.

But the recent history of vocational-technical high schools in Massachusetts reveals that the skills gap is really a gap in knowledge, and one that these schools have effectively closed in the last 25 years.

Perhaps the most transformative element of the state's landmark 1993 Education Reform Act was a requirement that voctech students be held to the same academic standards as their counterparts in comprehensive public high schools, including that they pass the same tests to achieve their diplomas.

The sharp distinction that once existed between college-bound students from comprehensive schools and voc-tech students heading straight for a blue-collar job in a factory or garage has been largely erased.

Today, thanks to years of hard work and strategic thinking, voc-tech schools have become schools of choice across Massachusetts. Often, graduates do bring muscle and dexterity to their careers, but, more importantly, all exhibit the strengths of mind and character that the great Roman orator Cicero identified more than 2,000 years ago as the keys to great achievement.

Embracing Rigorous Standards Across the Curriculum

To their credit, voc-tech leaders in the 1990s overcame their initial doubts about their students' ability to achieve on a par with their peers in conventional "academic" schools. They decided to embrace rigorous academic standards and accountability. They worked tirelessly to forge strong partnerships with local employers.

Even while retaining their traditional focus on trades and careers, voc-tech schools have embraced the liberal arts. Studying the works of Shakespeare, for example, has enabled voc-tech students to match the performance of their peers at comprehensive high schools on state tests. And the Bay State sets a high standard: Massachusetts students have placed first in the nation in each subject and on every grade level in all but one administration of the National Assessment of Educational Progress since 2005.

The embrace of a truly holistic curriculum has paid handsome dividends. Voc-tech schools have succeeded in closing both the knowledge gap that has long concerned employers and the achievement gaps of perennial concern to educators, parents, and taxpayers.

Voc-Tech Is Succeeding by Every Measure

Today's voc-tech students have lower dropout rates than their counterparts at comprehensive high schools. They pass the same academic tests required for graduation while adding practical life skills in a chosen career. And voc-tech schools excel while having higher-than-average percentages of low-income and special needs students.

Two-thirds of today's voc-tech graduates go on to post-secondary education. And a survey conducted by the Dukakis Center at Northeastern University found that the one-third of voc-tech graduates who enter the workforce directly after receiving their diploma are more job-ready than other high school graduates.

Unsurprisingly, the achievements of voc-tech schools across Massachusetts have led to increased demand. There are now about 5,000 more students who would like to attend a voc-tech in Massachusetts than there are available seats, a situation explored at length in this book.

Putting Competence Before Soft Skills and Fads

The success of Massachusetts's voc-tech schools vindicates the work of University of Virginia Professor Emeritus E.D. Hirsch Jr., who has long argued persuasively for the primacy of imparting academic knowledge in public education.

The Education Reform Act prioritized core academics. It eschewed soft skills such as "cultural competence" and "global awareness" in favor of a strong focus on the liberal arts, including history and literature, and enforcing accountability through high-stakes testing.

Going forward, the challenge will be to protect this focus on knowledge and accountability from the many fads that mark modern education, including "21st century skills," "social emotional learning," and efforts to move away from objective assessment.

In just the last few years, with apparent disregard for their remarkable track record of success, voc-tech schools in Massachusetts have been subjected to new admissions procedures that threaten to undermine the very principles driving their success.

The new guidelines, for example, bar schools from considering applicants' full attendance and disciplinary records — excusing allegedly minor infractions. Yet habits of attendance and behavior have been essential to driving down dropout rates and fostering in students the very habits of mind and work that employers prize.

The Freedom to Choose Schools of Choice

It is vital to recognize that voc-tech high schools in the Bay State today are truly schools of choice. The tens of thousands of students who attend them do so not because they are assigned to them by accident of birth, place of residence, or some administrator's decision, but because they want to be there.

In this respect, vocational education throughout the United States has long been different from that found in European countries, where students are directed onto a particular career path. This right to self-determination promotes social mobility and is at the heart of American democracy.

At the same time, policy makers and the public must remember that these schools are not for everyone. To ensure their continued success, they must be reserved for students whose families actively choose this type of education or career pathway.

The success of voc-tech education in Massachusetts proves that the much-discussed skills gaps really is a knowledge gap, and one that vocational schools have helped close for a generation now. Ensuring that these schools continue to do precisely that means protecting the foundations of their success — a rigorous vocational and liberal arts education, strong accountability measures, and independent governance.

■ ■ ■

Thomas F. Birmingham is the former Massachusetts Senate president and the distinguished senior fellow in education at Pioneer Institute in Boston.

William F. Weld was governor of Massachusetts from 1991 until 1997 and is a lawyer in Boston.

Introduction

Hands, Hearts, and Minds: The Promise of Vocational-Technical Education

by Jacqueline M. Moore

Vocational-technical education, once known as industrial education, began in 1830s America, when many reformers believed that teaching additional skills to working-class Americans would help them escape poverty.

Many nineteenth-century Americans thought certain groups—including African Americans, Native Americans, and poor whites—were not capable of learning. Some factory owners, for example, expected that vocational and industrial education would simply teach obedience and morality and help farmhands and rural employees improve their punctuality.

But social reformers and minority activists of all races, along with more forward-thinking business owners and educators, recognized that teaching workers practical skills would help American economic development. They campaigned tirelessly to help change attitudes and laws throughout the nation.

The most significant of these laws, the Morrill Land-Grant Acts of 1862, established colleges whose purpose was "... to teach such branches of learning as are related to agriculture and the mechanic arts... in order to promote the liberal and practical education of the industrial classes."

Debating an Educational Legacy

Despite steady growth and success of vocational education over nearly two centuries, some still question its value, even in Massachusetts, long an educational pioneer.

From Harvard College to Horace Mann, the Bay State's commitment to comprehensive education—literacy, history, arts, sciences, and languages—is unmatched.

But Massachusetts also boasts a strong network of agricultural, technical, and vocational schools that combine Yankee practicality with high-tech know-how to offer extraordinary educational options for a new century.

With this book, Pioneer Institute spotlights the history, status, and growing importance of voc-tech education. This is an area in which the Bay State has become a national leader, weaving together occupational education with a rigorous academic curriculum grounded in the liberal arts.

Two Extraordinary Lives

One of the most engaging ways to understand the history and development of voc-tech is through the lives and words of two extraordinary Americans—Booker T. Washington and W.E.B. Du Bois.

Both men held passionate and often divergent views about education. Both had strong ties to Massachusetts. And while neither's vision fully prevailed, both helped shape the historical debate that has yielded extraordinarily rich choices for today's students—in both vocational and comprehensive schools, and particularly in Massachusetts.

Booker T. Washington: Up from Slavery

Born into slavery in Virginia in 1856, Booker T. Washington grew up in poverty—and driven by a desire to read. As he recalls in *Up from Slavery*, his mother "procured an old copy of Webster's 'blue-back' spelling-book" from which he taught himself the alphabet.

In 1872, helped by donations from his hometown, Washington

traveled hundreds of miles to reach Virginia's Hampton Normal and Agricultural Institute. There, a skeptical head teacher gave him the chance to prove himself by cleaning the school's recitation room. He passed with flying colors.

Hampton taught its students practical trades as well as basic academics, and Washington's years there convinced him that industrial education provided unique opportunities for poor African Americans.

In 1881, Hampton President Samuel C. Armstrong recommended Washington, now 25, to lead a new industrial education school in Tuskegee, Alabama.

Starting with just $2,000, Washington and Black residents of the town literally built a school—making bricks, constructing buildings, growing crops, and raising livestock. Tuskegee became a model of scientific industrial education for African Americans.

Washington led Tuskegee for 30 years, gained the support and admiration of white philanthropists and politicians, and became the nation's foremost Black leader.

W.E.B. Du Bois: Forging the Souls of Black Folk

W.E.B. Du Bois was born poor but free in 1868 in Great Barrington, Massachusetts. He attended school with white children and worked throughout high school, shoveling coal, mowing lawns, and delivering newspapers. He took college-preparatory courses, including algebra, Greek, and Latin.

While many of Du Bois's classmates went on to Harvard, he went to an historically Black college—Fisk University in Nashville, Tennessee.

In Tennessee, Du Bois first experienced racism and segregation on a daily basis. In the summer breaks he taught rural sharecroppers and saw how difficult it was for them to get ahead.

Shaped by those experiences, Du Bois resolved to obtain an advanced degree in sociology to show the true impact of racism, and, in 1895, became the first African American to receive a Ph.D. from Harvard.

At just 29, Du Bois joined the faculty at Atlanta University where he started the Sociology Department. He helped found the American Negro Academy and, between 1898 and 1913, published reports on economic and social conditions in Black communities.

He also began to develop his ideas about the "talented tenth," declaring in a 1903 essay that "The Negro race, like all races, is going to be saved by its exceptional men."

Divergent Paths Toward a Common Goal

In the late 1890s and early 1900s, Du Bois and Washington worked together to establish the National Negro Business League, to stop a Georgia amendment that would have disenfranchised Black voters, and to challenge segregation on interstate trains.

But the men also had differences.

Washington never doubted the industrial education model pioneered at the Hampton Institute. He built Tuskegee on that model and won support from Black and white donors of all economic classes.

Du Bois acknowledged Washington's achievements but concluded that African Americans, however hardworking, would continue to be held back by racism in a segregated society. He became increasingly committed to protests, social activism, and legal action.

A Split Over the "Atlanta Compromise"

In 1895, Washington had delivered a key address to the Atlanta Cotton States and International Exposition. Stressing hard work and gradual progress, he argued Blacks should "cast down their buckets" in agriculture, mechanics, commerce, domestic service, and other professions.

"No race can prosper till it learns that there is as much dignity in tilling a field as in writing a poem," he said. "It is at the bottom of life we must begin and not at the top. Nor should we permit our grievances to overshadow our opportunities."

Although well received by many—including President Grover Cleveland, the press, and many Southerners—others labeled Washington's speech the "Atlanta Compromise" and damaging to Black civil rights.

In his 1903 essay "On Booker T. Washington and Others," Du Bois accused Washington of sacrificing political power, civil rights, and higher education for Black youth.

The Debate Ensues: An Education in Trades or Classical Learning?

However public their disagreements, both men understood the need for both practical and classical education.

Washington incorporated liberal arts into the Tuskegee curriculum and sent his daughter, Portia, to Massachusetts to pursue classical education. She attended Framingham Normal School—now Framingham State University—and Wellesley College before graduating from the former Bradford Academy in Haverhill and becoming a pianist and music teacher.

Yet Washington also told cautionary tales about poor families who bought pianos rather than tools in an effort to seem more refined. And he often told white audiences about a poor sharecropper boy he found in a field reading a French grammar book, which Washington saw as ridiculous.

Du Bois did not object to industrial training and never expected all African Americans to get a college degree. But in that image of the boy reading French grammar, Du Bois saw hope and aspiration, even if that child would never attend college or visit France.

"The Talented Tenth"

Du Bois focused on training the "talented tenth" for positions of leadership. He worried that Washington's emphasis on industrial education would drain resources from schools, like Atlanta University, that emphasized a classical curriculum. Indeed, donations to these schools did decline, as Washington raised millions for industrial education for Blacks. In response, many Black universities began to offer more industrial training akin to that found at Tuskegee.

Washington insisted industrial education was the best way to fund Black education throughout the South. Du Bois saw it as a way for white Americans to limit African Americans to manual labor.

"I would not deny," he wrote in "The Talented Tenth" (1903) "… or seem to depreciate in the slightest degree the important part industrial schools must play in the accomplishment of these ends, but I *do* say, and insist upon it, that it is industrialism drunk with its vision of success, to imagine that its own work can be accomplished without providing for the training of broadly cultured men and women to teach its own teachers, and to the teachers of the public schools."

Trading a Myth for a Balanced Educational Vision

Unfortunately, the long debate between Washington and Du Bois left an enduring myth that classical and voc-tech education are in conflict.

That perception began to change when the Cold War, the space program, and the Computer Age highlighted a growing need for technical know-how and spurred growth of voc-tech schools.

Today, faced with complex social, economic, and environmental problems, parents, educators, and taxpayers recognize that we need both comprehensive and voc-tech educational models.

Seizing the Opportunities of Education Reform

The landmark 1993 Massachusetts Education Reform Act, with its focus on classical liberal arts state standards in English, mathematics, science, and history, helped inaugurate a new era of excellence throughout public schools in the Bay State.

Voc-tech schools have fully embraced these opportunities, having now spent nearly 30 years combining outstanding occupational education offerings with a deeper commitment to English, mathematics, and the sciences.

Balancing hands-on learning internships in the business community with a firm grounding in core academic areas, including the liberal arts, has fundamentally transformed technical education in the Commonwealth.

Massachusetts has become the unquestioned national leader in voc-tech education, and its students today are among the best prepared in the nation to compete in a global economy.

'Making America Stronger'

Nowhere has that understanding been more clearly demonstrated than in minority-majority school districts in Worcester and Springfield, both of which replaced aging voc-tech schools with new, state-of-the-art facilities during the last 15 years.

Springfield's Putnam Vocational Technical Academy opened its new building in 2012. And in Worcester, the city's aging trade school in Lincoln Square was replaced in 2006 with a new Worcester Technical High School on Skyline Drive.

Eight years later, on June 11, 2014, President Barack Obama was the keynote speaker at the school's commencement.

"I'm here today because there is nothing ordinary about Worcester Tech or the Class of 2014," Obama said. "You have set yourselves apart. This high school has set itself apart. Over the past four years, some of you have learned how to take apart an engine and put it back together again. Some of you have learned how to run a restaurant, or build a house, or fix a computer. And all of you are graduating today not just with a great education, but with the skills that will let you start your careers and skills that will make America stronger."

The Triumph of a Dual Legacy

Obama's words on that June day in Worcester underscore that the greatness of a nation depends upon maximizing educational opportunity for all.

Debates over school governance and funding will always be with us. But few today dispute that both hands-on skills and great literature, art, and music should be available to all. Extending opportunity beyond the ranks of the privileged and wealthy — even beyond Du Bois's "talented tenth" — is today understood as fundamentally American in character.

In the end, Washington and Du Bois both contributed to a shared understanding that is guiding a new birth of educational freedom. And their words — recorded at a time in our history still stained with prejudice and segregation — sound both prescient and hopeful to us today:

"A system of education is not one thing, nor does it have a single object," wrote Du Bois in 1903. "Education is that whole system of training within and without school house walls, which molds and develops men."

"There was never a time when I felt more hopeful for the race than I do at the present," wrote Washington in 1901. "The great human law that in the end recognizes and rewards merit is everlasting and universal."

■ ■ ■

Jacqueline M. Moore is a former Professor of History at Austin College and author of *Booker T. Washington, W.E.B. Du Bois, and the Struggle for Racial Equality* and *Leading the Race: The Black Elite in the Nation's Capital, 1880-1920*. She coedited the African American History Series for Rowman & Littlefield and received the T. R. Fehrenbach Book Award for *Cow Boys and Cattle Men: Class and Masculinities on the Texas Frontier, 1865-1900*, and was the 2015 CASE Professor of the Year for Texas. She has led workshops on pedagogy and effective teaching strategies. She was a Fulbright Scholar in Hong Kong, where she worked on general education reform for Hong Kong's higher education sector.

Chapter 1

Massachusetts: A Pioneer and Leader in Vocational-Technical Education

by Alison L. Fraser

Massachusetts, a pioneer in many ways, has always been at the forefront of vocational-technical education. In 1908, a bequest from Hatfield resident Oliver Smith established the Smith School in Northampton. Known today as Smith Vocational and Agricultural High School, it was the forerunner for a mode of education that remains vitally important to the state's workforce.

Massachusetts's vocational-technical schools offer a unique mix of academic, career, and extracurricular activities. These schools provide students throughout the state with both a comprehensive academic education and the skills and experience needed for outstanding employment opportunities.

There are 90 school districts across Massachusetts that offer vocational programs under Chapter 74 of state law, which governs vocational education. The range is from just one such program to as many as 29, but every student in the Commonwealth has access to one or more schools offering some form of vocational, technical, or agricultural curriculum.

The increasing popularity of these schools over the last 20 years means that there are often long waiting lists and specific entrance requirements for students who seek the voc-tech combination of rigorous academics and practical apprenticeships.

Voc-tech graduates leave high school better equipped for the workforce than many or most college-preparatory students. They are often praised by industry professionals as more prepared and capable for jobs where their skills and talents can be utilized to the fullest.

Initially opposed to education reform and higher academic standards, voc-tech educators over the last 25 years have come to see the advantages of accountability. They have embraced standards that have pushed their students to better-than-average graduation rates and scores on the Massachusetts Comprehensive Assessment System (MCAS) tests.

Today, two-thirds of voc-tech graduates pursue postsecondary education, and importantly, special education voc-tech students are counted among those with the highest graduation rates. Voc-tech dropout rates are significantly lower than state averages. In the 2018–2019 academic year, the latest for which the state has released data, the statewide dropout rate was 1.8 percent; the rate for all 41 of the state's voc-tech schools was 0.7 percent, and the rate among the 26 regional voc-tech schools was 0.6 percent.

These academic results reflect the combination of high expectations by educators and rigorous coursework by students. Intricate concepts are placed in a recognizable context through hands-on and demonstrative study. Academic and technical knowledge is integrated through practical applications that are tested in both the classroom and workshop. Voc-tech students graduate with a well-rounded understanding of how the knowledge they have gained can work for them.

Voc-tech education has succeeded through the combination of operational autonomy, choice, rigorous instruction, and relationships with local businesses. These are factors that any legislator or policy maker should be aware of when focusing on school reform.

Moreover, because voc-tech education serves disadvantaged

populations well, it should not only continue but be expanded in Massachusetts.

Introduction and History

According to the National Association of Manufacturers, just over 7 percent of Massachusetts's workforce is employed in manufacturing, creating $54.6 billion worth of goods annually as of 2019 and employing 236,000 people.

That makes manufacturing the state's fourth largest sector, behind health care, retail trade, and education. As the economy emerges from supply chain problems and labor shortages caused by the COVID-19 pandemic, the state projects significant growth across all labor sectors, including manufacturing.

According to the Department of Unemployment Assistance's Economic Research Department, overall employment in the state is expected to rise by 2.95 percent between 2018 and 2028.

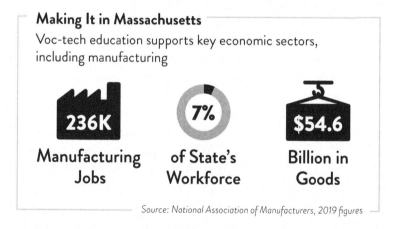

Making It in Massachusetts

Voc-tech education supports key economic sectors, including manufacturing

236K — Manufacturing Jobs

7% — of State's Workforce

$54.6 — Billion in Goods

Source: National Association of Manufacturers, 2019 figures

That includes approximately 4 percent increases in the numbers of first-line supervisors in both the construction trades and for supervision of production and operating workers, and a more than 8 percent increase in the numbers of plumbers, pipefitters, and steamfitters. Nursing, health care, food service, and computer science also are expected to post significant increases.[1]

Vocational education—with increased support, availability,

and corporate partnerships—is one important way that Massachusetts can prepare enough skilled workers in the years to come. As the nature of Massachusetts's manufacturing has changed over the last century from low technology to high technology, so has the nature of vocational schools. While they still offer carpentry, metal fabrication, plumbing, and advanced manufacturing, today's vocational students also study robotics, biotechnology, engineering technology, and electronics. The demand for higher skills in even the most conventional manufacturing jobs has meant higher expectations—and higher academic achievement—for the state's more than 50,000 voc-tech students.

Massachusetts: The 'Grandfather of Vocational Education'

On May 24, 1905, Massachusetts Governor William L. Douglas, a shoe manufacturer from Brockton, approved a legislative resolution establishing a commission to examine the nature of and the need for industrial education.

A year later, the Massachusetts Commission on Industrial and Technical Education filed a Senate bill titled An Act to Provide Further for Industrial Education.[2]

Enacted in June 1906 and amended in 1911 and 1921, this law made Massachusetts the "grandfather of vocational education."

According to state and federal definitions, voc-tech schools educate and prepare students for both employment and continuing academic and occupational training, by integrating academic and vocational education, following both the state's voc-tech education frameworks and curriculum frameworks. Their programs must include competency-based applied learning that contributes to students' academic knowledge, work attitudes, general employability skills, and the occupational-specific skills necessary for independence.

Funding for these schools comes from regional member districts, Chapter 70 state disbursements, and grants from the federal Carl D. Perkins Career and Technical Education Improvement Act (originally authorized in 1984), through which the federal government distributes almost $1.3 billion yearly to fund career and technical education programs in all 50 states.

The Voc-Tech Readiness Advantage

In 2006, the Massachusetts Business Alliance for Education (MBAE) released *Preparing for the Future: Employer Perspectives on Work Readiness Skills,*[3] a report to inform educators and policy makers about the work readiness skills that employers expect of Massachusetts high school graduates, and to describe the skills and characteristics corporations require for entry-level positions with potential for growth and advancement.

According to the report, of the dozens of professionals who participated in the study, "There was general agreement that vocational school graduates are more job-ready than general education or college preparatory high school graduates. In fact, a number of participants felt that vocational high school graduates were often more job-ready than college graduates."

Also, employers felt that vocational graduates are more team-oriented, disciplined, and prepared to enter the workforce. Graduates of vocational schools were described as having superior soft skills and preparation in comparison to other graduates.

High Schools of Choice

In 1962, a drive was begun to create regional voc-tech high schools across Massachusetts, resulting in 26 regional voc-tech schools joining three regional agricultural schools that had already been serving many communities for decades.

Each regional school is considered its own district, with a school committee and superintendent, and enjoying—within state frameworks, guidelines, and accountability measures—the ability to create its own curriculum and instructional policies and methods.

By law, each student in Massachusetts has access to either a regional or district vocational program. Eight of the larger districts in the state have voc-tech high schools within their local systems. These include Worcester Technical High School,

Madison Park Technical Vocational High School in Boston, and Roger L. Putnam Vocational Technical Academy in Springfield. In addition to the state's 26 regional voc-tech schools, Massachusetts has two county agricultural schools, one independent school, one CVTE (Career Vocational Technical Education) collaborative, and 41 districts that have Chapter 74 programs within their comprehensive high school.

Massachusetts students do not have to give up sports, electives, or—most importantly—a full academic program to pursue vocational education. Literally half the student's instructional time is spent in shop or career education. By contrast, vocational schools in the South run a six-period day, with one block called shop, much like an elective. Even neighboring New York's vocational system places the student in shop for just half a day at a time.

In Massachusetts, the model of long stretches of instructional time—a full week of academics alternating with a full week in shop—is considered vital for authentic learning.

All vocational teachers in Massachusetts must:

- Be licensed by the Massachusetts Department of Elementary and Secondary Education (DESE)
- Hold specific education credentials—an associate, bachelor's, or master's degree
- Hold state academic licenses in their field of instruction
- Have three to five years of experience in the field in which they are licensed
- Pass either the standard Massachusetts Tests for Educator Licensure (MTEL) Communication and Literary Skills Test
- Complete 18 college credits in vocational education courses approved by the state

In addition, for certain vocational fields, program instructors must obtain state, federal, and/or industry-issued licenses or certifications.

Changing the Mindset and Improving Results

Voc-tech schools understand that approximately 50 percent of Massachusetts high school students do not plan to enter a four-year college program after graduation. Indeed, most vocational students choose a two-year college or technical program, the military, or go directly into the workplace. Nonetheless, voc-tech schools hold their students to the same high academic standards that students who attend comprehensive high schools must meet.

Today's pragmatic students are increasingly eager to acquire real-world skills and get an early start on career training, particularly with ever-increasing college costs. Vocational schools also offer a wider slate of attractive career programs, outfitting shops with the latest equipment that simulates actual professional conditions.

Nationwide, enrollment in career and technical education, both secondary and postsecondary, rose 57 percent between 2000 and 2004. Fifteen years later, by the 2019–2020 academic year, there were 11.1 million students participating in career and vocational education at some level across the nation—7.6 million at the secondary level and 3.5 million at the postsecondary level, according to data from the U.S. Department of Education.[4]

Growing Popularity Creates Waiting Lists

Along with traditional trades such as carpentry, cosmetology, and plumbing, voc-tech schools offer telecommunications, networking, computer repair, Allied Health, environmental technology, and pre-engineering programs.

Vocational educators recognize that even traditional trades today require a higher level of academic knowledge.

As voc-tech schools have embraced higher academic standards and expanded their offerings, they have grown in popularity. And since they are today schools of choice, applications far exceed the number of available seats, despite an increase in capacity in many of the schools. As a result, virtually all the state's voc-tech schools have had significant waiting lists in recent years.

This is particularly true in the state's Gateway Cities — including Lowell, Fall River, Worcester, Springfield, and Pittsfield. These and similar cities were defined in a 2007 Brookings Institution report as midsized urban centers that anchor regional economies, possess unrealized potential, and face "stubborn social and economic challenges."[5]

A strong need exists to expand the number of Chapter 74 seats to meet demand, both in Gateway Cities and elsewhere, but financial restrictions make further expansion very difficult. Instead, a new set of regulations to guide the voc-tech admissions process governs how students are selected for admission.

The Revised Voc-Tech Application Process

The application process for vocational and agricultural schools may include rubrics for scholarship (including successful completion of the sending grade), number of unexcused absences, discipline, and recommendations from the sending school. Most also require an interview.

All career voc-tech schools and programs approved under Chapter 74 must:

- Admit resident students who meet the minimum requirements for admission prior to accepting non-resident students seeking the same program
- Condition admission on a student successfully being promoted to the grade for which they have won admission
- Include a description of the process for application and admission to the school, as well as admission to programs within the school, including any criteria, lotteries, or other processes to be used in selecting students
- Develop a plan that includes deliberate, specific strategies to promote equal educational opportunities and attract, enroll, and retain a student population that, when compared to students in similar grades in sending districts, has a comparable academic and demographic profile

In addition to what Chapter 74 schools are required to do,

the state lists prohibited practices:

- Career voc-tech schools and programs that use selective criteria for admissions must not use criteria that have the effect of disproportionately excluding persons of a particular race, color, national origin, sex, gender identity, sexual orientation, religion, or disability unless they demonstrate that such criteria have been validated as essential to participation in vocational programs, and alternative equally valid criteria that do not have such a disproportionate adverse effect are unavailable.

- These schools cannot consider excused absences in the review of attendance records.

- When reviewing discipline records, these schools cannot consider a student's minor behavior or disciplinary infractions. This means schools and programs cannot consider any student conduct other than infractions that resulted in suspensions or expulsion under specific sections of Massachusetts General Laws Chapter 71.

Embracing Higher Academic Standards

Vocational school leaders recognized that education research supported the conclusion that the academic skills needed for entry-level career success are equal to those needed for college entrance.

The manuals used by professional plumbers, major appliance repair personnel, auto mechanics, and other professionals in the trades are written at up to a grade 14 reading level.

The shift at voc-tech schools to place substantially greater emphasis on academics was motivated in part by the arrival of MCAS testing. Although the academic standards mandated by the Massachusetts Education Reform Act of 1993 were originally resisted by the administrators of most voc-tech schools, those administrators have since come to embrace the state's rigorous academic standards.

An early acceptance of the inevitability and usefulness of

MCAS made Blackstone Valley Tech—located in Upton and serving 13 communities—the first vocational school where 100 percent of its students passed MCAS to graduate.

An administrator at Blue Hills Regional Technical School in Canton said, "MCAS really did us a favor, because now every high school in the Commonwealth is on a level playing field."

And Eugene Carlo, the superintendent at Assabet Valley Regional Technical High School in Marlborough, who had been a vocal opponent of the state standards and assessments in the 1990s, publicly declared at a Massachusetts Business Alliance for Education event in 2006 that "MCAS was the best thing that ever happened to us."

Sustaining Improvement in Academics

This shift in priorities led to a long-term, sustained improvement in academic performance at voc-tech schools. Among the class of 2008, for example, 96 percent of students passed both the math and English portions of the MCAS, beating out the statewide average of 94 percent. Further, the average graduation rate at regional voc-tech schools that year was almost 10 points higher than the state average—90.5 percent compared to 80.9 percent.[6]

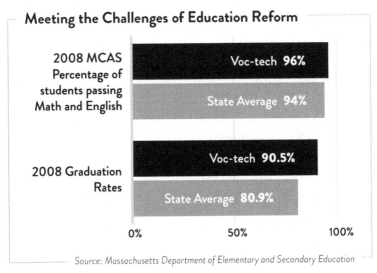

Meeting the Challenges of Education Reform

2008 MCAS Percentage of students passing Math and English

Voc-tech **96%**

State Average **94%**

2008 Graduation Rates

Voc-tech **90.5%**

State Average **80.9%**

0%　　　　50%　　　　100%

Source: Massachusetts Department of Elementary and Secondary Education

In the years since, graduation rates have continued to increase statewide for both voc-tech and comprehensive high schools. The nearly 10-point gap seen in 2008 has narrowed significantly, indicating that overall performance has been improving across the broader public school system — including voc-tech and comprehensive schools alike.

Testing Incoming Freshmen Leads to Success

Blackstone Valley Tech has one of the most extensive programs for bringing up the academic levels of their students. Recognizing that one in four students enters their freshman year with a fourth grade reading level, they test every student before matriculation, and everyone who is below grade level is placed in an individualized remediation program until he or she is reading at grade level.

As part of their focus on academic and MCAS success, the administration also increased the length of math and English blocks, and gradually increased the length of the school year by 15 days to 195 days. All of this has made a tremendous difference in academic performance for Valley Tech students.

Norfolk Agricultural Technical School is another institution that has successfully embraced academic as well as professional improvement for its students. Since 2002, Norfolk Agricultural has emphasized integration of academic and vocational education. Sessions now link dairy processing with chemical biotechnology, garden design with measurement skills, and diesel mechanics with earth science. Every instructor on the vocational side has created at least one lesson in partnership with an academic teacher.

Successes like these have repositioned vocational schools as schools of choice for students desiring a technical background who are likely to go on to postsecondary education.

Closing Performance and Attendance Gaps

For instance, at Old Colony Regional Vocational Technical High School in Rochester, 100 percent of students who took

MCAS last year passed, and 60 percent of graduates continued their studies at the postsecondary level.

Since 2018, 100 percent of each senior class at Essex North Shore Agricultural & Technical High School in Danvers have met the MCAS Competency Determination for graduation. According to postsecondary enrollment reports posted by DESE, 207 of the school's 2019 graduates (64.5 percent) enrolled in postsecondary education.

Overall, the 26 regional vocational and three agricultural schools have achieved an average 42 percent on Massachusetts's Composite Performance Index (a measure of the extent to which students in a group are progressing toward proficiency) since 2001 — ranging from +17.4 percent at Minuteman Regional Vocational Technical High School in Lexington to +83.1 percent at Whittier Regional Vocational Technical High School in Haverhill.

The combined Average Performance Index of 81.7 points for these schools is close to the statewide average of 86.5 points.

The achievement gap between vocational and comprehensive high schools narrowed by 27 percent in six years, helping drive down the voc-tech dropout rate to just 1.5 percent, compared to 3.8 percent statewide.

More recently, voc-tech schools across the state have continued to reduce dropout rates. Four regional schools — Blue Hills, Montachusett Regional Vocational Technical School in Fitchburg, Shawsheen Valley Technical High School in Billerica, and Tri-County Regional Vocational Technical High School in Franklin — have a dropout rate of just 0.1 percent. And both Bristol County Agricultural High School in Dighton and Blackstone Valley Tech had zero dropouts in the last academic year.

Teaching Shakespeare and More

One of the most difficult but important conditions needed for success is to raise teacher and staff expectations for all students. Researchers have discovered that when teachers see themselves as teaching extraordinarily difficult-to-teach students, they perceive a lack of efficacy and lose their motivation.

Conversely, when teachers hold high expectations for students, that feeling is communicated to the pupils, who "…are likely to achieve at higher levels than are students who sense that their teacher considers them unable to master the work."[7]

"We are definitely ratcheting up expectations," an administrator at Assabet Valley said. "In the past, we didn't teach Shakespeare, for instance. Even a recent MCAS alternative assessment was on *Romeo and Juliet*, so if you've never been exposed to it, and you're not used to talking about plot and theme and character, because they're busy giving you elementary reading, then you haven't got a chance. The interesting thing is that when you do the higher order stuff the right way with these kids, they love it, and they succeed."

The superintendent at South Shore Regional Vocational Technical High School in Hanover explained: "We've made tremendous strides in improving the academic side of the house, and there has been a general trend toward the realization that a truly prepared craftsman really needs a balanced portfolio of skills. Vocational schools can no longer be viewed as terminal points for education. This can truly be a dual-preparation high school process."[8]

AP Courses and Apprenticeships

Many vocational schools now offer Advanced Placement (AP) classes for their students. And Assabet Valley was one of five high schools in the pilot year of the Massachusetts State Scholars Initiative—a program to prepare students for postsecondary success by pursuing a rigorous high school curriculum, including AP courses.

A standard part of the voc-tech experience is the co-op, where qualified juniors and seniors spend what would be their shop weeks working, for pay, at a real job in their fields of study, to supplement their formal instruction.[9]

Also available to vocational students are formal articulation agreements with the trades' registered apprenticeship programs. These programs have recognized the high caliber of voc-tech education by accepting qualified voc-tech graduates into programs that offer a full-time job in their fields, a master tradesman as a mentor, and support for one to two college courses per year.

Requiring MassCore Coursework

Massachusetts's vocational schools have also been ahead of the pack in requiring all students to complete what has become the recommended MassCore of high school coursework.

That consists of four credits of English, four credits of math, three credits of lab-based science, three credits of history and social science, and two credits of the same foreign language — although most vocational schools make foreign language study optional.

In addition, the MassCore standard requires schools provide additional learning opportunities, including AP classes, dual enrollment, a senior project, online courses for high school or college credit, and service or work-based learning.

Remembering Socio-Cultural Context

Because of the perceived blue-collar nature of study in voc-tech schools — and the perception that academic teachers come from white-collar backgrounds — a cultural divide can open between teachers and students.

The embrace of higher expectations for students and the integration of academic skills into vocational shops are two key factors that can help guard against such a divide.

Mary Metz's work on how social class differences shape teachers' work demonstrated that students themselves often introduce class issues into schools but advised that faculty and administrators must not reinforce these feelings by teaching down to them.

Metz warned that no matter what the socioeconomic status of students or instructors, "Schools should be places to create the curious, informed and responsible citizen, rather than the ready occupant of an occupational slot."[10]

Success with Students with Special Needs

Massachusetts's regional vocational schools also have excellent success with their students with special needs, even though their populations of students with Individualized Education Programs (IEPs) are significantly higher than the state average.

The average percentage of special needs students in the state is 18.7 percent, whereas the average percentage of students with special needs in the regional vocational schools is 22.5 percent, with four schools having greater than 30 percent of their students on IEPs, ranging up to 44.1 percent special needs students at Minuteman.

Nonetheless, the 88 percent graduation rate of special needs students at vocational schools is significantly higher than the state average for special needs students of 73.9 percent.

Because of the larger number of students with special needs, voc-tech schools have created programs that are not usually available in other high schools.

Reading and mathematics classes, for example, are taught by specialists who combine classroom and laboratory instruction with specialized software packages. Once students have improved their skills, they are transitioned into mainstream courses as soon as possible.

Concepts in Context

Students at vocational schools report that they want to do more than just "sit in a classroom." They appreciate the opportunity to learn by doing, and to understand deeply what Blue Hills teachers call "concepts in context"—like learning physics by studying how hydraulic brakes work or knowing how to correctly frame a house because of a thorough understanding of the Pythagorean theorem.[11]

David Hawkins, in his essay, *I, Thou, and It*, might have been describing vocational education when he praised that "third thing which is of interest to the child and to the adult, in which they can join in outward projection."[12]

That third thing—that "it"—is the in-depth study of skills

that is the basis for career and technical education. Vocational education supports the philosophy that many students learn more effectively within a real-world context.[13]

The Role of Advisory Committees

Every voc-tech school has a General Advisory Committee, consisting of the chairs of each of a school's Program Advisory Committees. The general committee exists, according to Chapter 74 regulations, to "advise the school committee, based on adequate and timely information, as to the planning, operation, and evaluation of vocational technical instruction provided by programs under its control."

In addition, state regulations require that each vocational program has industry professionals who advise instructors on the skills that will be most marketable for graduates in consideration of workforce and job market trends, technology, and training.

Some Shops Welcome the Public

Along with the advisory committees, vocational and agricultural technical schools have deep and useful ties to their communities. For example, the auto body and auto shops are open for residents to use for car repairs, and the cosmetology shops have regular days when they are open to the public. District schools and municipal governments use the talents and equipment of the graphics and print shops for their printing needs.

When the public uses these services, they pay for material costs, but not for labor. Every voc-tech school with a culinary arts program has a restaurant that is open to the public, whose waiting lines are testament to the excellent quality of the food and service provided by the chefs-in-training. One famous alumnus of these programs is Emeril Lagasse, who learned to work effectively in a kitchen at Diman Regional Vocational Technical High School in Fall River.

Gaining Experience in Local Communities

Students in many shops go off-site often, to share their skills with the community and to get practice working in real-life settings. The health professions students rotate through area nursing homes, hospitals, and clinics, while the construction cluster students build, renovate, and improve both municipal and nonprofit properties.

Students from facilities maintenance programs regularly ply their trade not only by maintaining the interiors and exteriors of their own schools, but through the design, planting, and upkeep of public properties. Likewise, much of the interior and exterior painting of public buildings is done by students in the painting and design shops, and they learn about historical decoration by working on historic churches and other buildings.

The professional-grade work of the students in the carpentry shops may be viewed and enjoyed throughout the Commonwealth in gazebos, bandstands, picnic groves, and boathouses, along with cabins, lodges, and other buildings at scout camps.

Often, several programs will work together to complete large projects. For example, when Blackstone Valley Tech built a new school facility, their own student electricians, plumbers, carpenters, metal fabricators, painters, and HVAC technicians worked alongside the subcontractors.

In Marlborough, the students in the construction cluster from Assabet Valley completed the redesign and renovation of the city's former central fire station for use as exhibition and office space.

Situated Learning and Cognitive Apprenticeships

The key to this system is situated learning, what Brown, Collins and Duguid, in their study "Situated Cognition and the Culture of Learning," describe as cognitive apprenticeship.[14]

The theory holds that teachers first "make explicit their tacit knowledge," then model its use in authentic activities, then support and finally empower the students to use that knowledge in independent authentic activities.

The term "student centered" is widespread in the literature of school reform, but one rarely encounters a clear definition. In voc-tech, however, it means that teachers are forced to do more than lecture and are encouraged to take on the role of instructional coach.

A 1998 survey conducted by the High Schools That Work program, under the aegis of the Southern Regional Education Board, found that students at vocational schools that showed dramatic improvements indicated key roles for cooperative learning, laboratory activities, student participation in decisions about achievement goals, mathematical models, and the creation of products to demonstrate their expertise.

In that same survey, teachers cited several factors in their growing success:

- Engaging students in learning activities that involve academic content
- Using manipulatives and hands-on experiments or projects to make content more concrete
- Having students do joint assignments in which they work with an academic and a vocational teacher
- Having students write in shop to clarify and communicate their ideas
- Increasing the numbers of students using mathematics to solve real-world problems
- Assigning more reading
- Encouraging students to take greater responsibility for their learning

Student Products and Performances

Because of the hands-on nature of vocational education, the creation of products and demonstrations should be a natural phenomenon, but it must be encouraged. One method for this encouragement is to offer activities and opportunities that will prepare the students from the time they arrive at high school for a major project in their senior year.

A majority of vocational schools in Massachusetts require that students produce a senior project and/or a portfolio in order to graduate. While such activities are common in many school-reform programs, the senior project takes on greater significance in career or vocational education, where students who have spent four years developing their expertise have the chance to display what they have accomplished.

Senior projects may include in-depth research, demonstrate problem solving, decision-making, and independent learning skills. Most importantly, these projects demonstrate to students and their communities how voc-tech education has given them the tools they need to create and provide professional products and services.[15]

After selecting a topic, the student conducts research, keeps a portfolio, and meets throughout the year with a senior project advisor and perhaps a project mentor from the community. Finally, the student produces a product and makes a formal presentation to teachers and community leaders, who ask questions and review the student's portfolio.

This process becomes an authentic assessment tool that teaches students about planning, deadlines, and project management. It offers opportunities to integrate academic and vocational studies, develop verbal and nonverbal communication skills, and feel a sense of accomplishment and camaraderie — or sometimes commiseration — with fellow seniors.

The project system fosters a collegial atmosphere among faculty and the professional community when, on demonstration day, they all come together to judge and to celebrate the accomplishments of their seniors. The senior capstone project, a culmination of the students' four years of academic and vocational studies, is a way for them to go out with a bang instead of a fizzle, as well as being an inspiration for students to continue with rigorous studies after they have successfully completed their MCAS requirements in 10th grade.

Integrating Academic and Technical Studies

Some vocational schools use cross-visitation among academic and vocational teachers for professional development. Academic teachers who visit shops can observe how their students, even those they had thought of as troublesome, may behave differently. When academic teachers observe students whom they had held in low esteem in their classrooms easily take apart and reassemble a freezer, or machine a set of tools, or expertly perform cardiopulmonary resuscitation (CPR), their impression changes and their expectations are raised.

One of the top voc-tech schools in the state, Blackstone Valley Tech, is an example of excellent academic-vocational integration.

Valley Tech assembled multidisciplinary teams that evaluated MCAS data and student weaknesses to identify areas in need of improvement. The teams then created teacher toolboxes to address those weak areas, including a how-to section on basic skills, practice problems and exercises for rote skills, and concrete applications for integration into other subjects.

Teachers worked together. For example, proportions might be reinforced in auto shop with algebra problems asking students to figure the rate at which a car is burning oil or losing tire tread, and a machine shop instructor might ask students for daily, written reflections on their work.

The toolbox is a way of bringing together all instructional staff and giving them a common language.

Occupational Proficiency

As another means of ensuring that voc-tech students are prepared to meet the needs of today's workplace, schools employ competency tracking systems that electronically keep tabs on students' portfolios and allow teachers to keep records of students' progress at meeting benchmarks.

Occupational major frameworks cover 45 separate career curricula and include all the skills learned within a specific program. Each of the career curricula contains four common strands: Health and Safety, Employability, Management and Entrepreneurship, and Underlying Principles of Technology.

A fifth strand is industry-validated and integrates embedded academic knowledge, skills, and competencies. It also refers instructors to the previously released Massachusetts Curriculum Frameworks in Arts, English Language Arts, Foreign Languages,

Comprehensive Health, Mathematics, History and Social Science, as well as Science and Technology/Engineering.

The frameworks offer detailed guidance for education professionals, including sample performance tasks and indicators, and resources (including call numbers for books, binders, and videos) that address each standard.

Each vocational framework:

- Includes the recommended sequence for acquisition of the knowledge, skills, and competencies in each strand and the recommended industry standards and student credentials for the program
- Helps ensure alignment to a common voc-tech curriculum format, thus allowing transferability among programs statewide, as well as use of common terms, goals, and program elements
- Legitimizes vocational programs, putting them on an equal footing with the state's long-established academic frameworks

Moreover, during the last four years, the Massachusetts Association of Vocational Administrators (MAVA), with funding from the DESE, has been updating all the voc-tech frameworks.

Financing Vocational-Technical Education

Funding Begins with Local Communities

Expenditures for voc-tech schools in Massachusetts are generally higher than at comprehensive high schools. They average $22,427 per pupil, ranging from $19,100 at Bay Path Regional Vocational Technical High School in Charlton to $34,100 at Minuteman.

Regional vocational districts are primarily funded through assessments based on attendance from the member communities in each region, Chapter 70 state funding, a Perkins allocation, and other grants. In addition, they may receive nonresident tuition (averaging $17,084), and fees earned from programs offered to the public, such as evening adult education and postsecondary career and technical programs.

During budget season, voc-tech superintendents must meet with the finance committees, city councils, and/or town meetings of each member community in their district, to justify the municipal assessments that support their budgets. This can mean negotiating with as many as a dozen municipalities simultaneously.

Technological Needs Increase Costs

The higher costs at voc-tech schools are in part due to the significantly higher special education populations in these schools. However, the main reason for costs exceeding the average statewide academic per-pupil expenditure is that vocational schools must equip their shops with the sophisticated technical equipment needed to assure training to industry standards.

These costs are often offset by in-kind contributions to the career and technical programs by those industries that will benefit from the special training of these schools' graduates.

For example, in the fall of 2021, Southwestern Industries, Inc. donated three new CNC TRAK-K3 mills to the Advanced Manufacturing Program at Old Colony Regional. The equipment, controls, installation, and instructor training are valued at $81,220.

The Massachusetts Workforce Skills Cabinet

The state's Workforce Skills Cabinet was created by an executive order of Governor Charlie Baker on February 26, 2015. The Cabinet aligns the Executive Offices of Education, Labor and Workforce Development, and Housing and Economic Development to develop a comprehensive economic growth agenda.

The WSC's Skills Capital Grant Program awards grants for the purchase and installation of equipment and related improvements and renovations necessary for installation and use of such equipment to support vocational and technical training. This equipment has upgraded and has expanded career technical education and training programs that are aligned to regional economic and workforce development priorities for in-demand industries.

The Capital Skills Grant Program has been a tremendous funding source for updating and adding needed equipment for voc-tech schools. From March 2017 through August 2021, Chapter 74 vocational-technical schools were awarded more than $30.6 million in funding. In addition, there has been $2.1 million for the Career Technical Initiative for Adult Leaners in voc-tech schools.

The Federal Perkins Act

The Carl D. Perkins Career and Technical Education Improvement Act of 2006 — known as Perkins IV — is a federal funding program administered by state education agencies. In 2007, Massachusetts disbursed nearly $18.4 million to Chapter 74 schools and two-year postsecondary career and technical programs.

The Perkins legislation was reauthorized in 2018 as the Strengthening Career and Technical Education Act for the 21st Century (Perkins V) Act. Massachusetts's total Perkins allocation for FY2021 was $21,740,338.

The most recent Perkins funding saw more than $12.4 million distributed to secondary voc-tech education, with 96 districts and communities receiving funds. The average award was $129,854, ranging from a low of $8,566 for Gateway Regional School District in the Berkshires to a high of $1,821,938 for Boston.

Vocational programs eligible for Perkins funds must offer coherent and rigorous content aligned with challenging standards and relevant technical knowledge and skills needed to prepare for further education and careers.

The programs must include competency-based applied learning, occupational safety and health, management and entrepreneurship knowledge and skills, and computer skills.

Conclusions and Implications

There are tremendous lessons to be learned from voc-tech education in Massachusetts. The achievements and contributions of these schools set examples that should be studied as some of the most successful models of high school design.

As has been demonstrated, the unique combination of increased academic expectations and professional-level occupational training unite to make the century-old history of Massachusetts voc-tech education a true American success story.

- Since 1962, regional voc-tech schools have been models of how diverse communities create efficient, regional educational institutions. The state's agricultural schools date back even further.

- As Massachusetts educators have begun to look at supplementing MCAS, they have the voc-tech senior project programs as a model.

- Voc-tech schools have demonstrated remarkable success with hard-to-serve populations, offering an excellent model for low-performing schools.

- District high schools that have Chapter 74 programs can, where necessary, use the models of high-performing regional voc-tech schools to improve their own programs.

- Urban centers should consider opening charter high schools based on the voc-tech and career education model.

- The autonomy of regional voc-tech schools is key to their success, suggesting that voc-tech schools imbedded in urban districts should be given similar autonomy.

- Voc-tech schools' success should encourage the creation of specialized programs for students with other talents and interests, such as in the visual and performing arts.

- Voc-tech schools enjoy enviable relationships with businesses, both in resource development and as advisors on the skills and knowledge that employers are seeking in Massachusetts's high school graduates.

■ ■ ■

Alison L. Fraser is an education policy, research, and strategy consultant and president of Practical Policy. Previously, she was an administrator at Blackstone Valley Tech and director of policy and advocacy at Mass Insight Education, where she directed the Great Schools Campaign and development of No Excuses for Failing Schools and Excellence in Math and Science Goals. An expert in standards-based curriculum, Fraser has coordinated activities and programs for the Coalition for Higher Standards and led research in standards-based reform.

Chapter 2

Filling the Skills Gap: Massachusetts's Vocational-Technical Schools and Business Partnerships

by Alison L. Fraser and William Donovan

Steadily, by economic necessity, a change is taking place in our society. The belief that a young person must obtain a college degree in something—anything—is giving ground to the necessity for a person to acquire skills. The recognition of the value of career voc-tech education is on the rise.

Society is recognizing that in today's economy, students from voc-tech schools are finding high-skill, high-wage jobs on par with—and sometimes ahead of—graduates of four-year liberal arts colleges. Why? Because they have marketable, industry-sanctioned competencies and employable skills.

The skilled labor shortage is a real problem for manufacturers, builders, and technical service providers—and has only been exacerbated by the COVID-19 pandemic. Many businesses are losing experienced employees to retirement and struggling to find qualified replacements. As their costs for training rise, their ability to expand is constrained, and their ability to compete is weakened, those employers are turning to voc-tech schools to remain viable.

Much as professional baseball teams have Triple-A affiliates for promising players, companies are investing in voc-tech schools to help train their future employees. They're creating a pipeline for talent by providing schools with the latest equipment and software, helping to finance new facilities, and partnering in co-op programs. Many voc-tech graduates move directly from their high school co-op experience into the local workforce, sometimes at the very companies where they enjoyed a co-op.

Voc-tech schools naturally welcome the investment as it enables them to keep pace with changes in the workplace, which are rapid and dramatic. Automotive technicians, to name just one vocation, aren't "gearheads" in the garage any longer. There is less turning of wrenches in the job and more analyzing the sophistication of the computerized diagnostic equipment that goes into it.

Through partnerships with employers, voc-tech schools become more vital contributors to the regional economy. The skills they teach in computer-aided design or machine technology can help fill openings among local plastics manufacturers in western Massachusetts. Creating a first-of-its-kind aviation program can train students for opportunities in the aviation cluster in the Pioneer Valley. And the training students receive on new computer-controlled lathes and milling machines enables them to step into jobs at the machine shops of Franklin County or in the Blackstone Valley.

These students aren't trained to be $600,000-per-year surgeons. But if they can master the software used on a factory floor or become a trained engineer or bio-technician, they can earn an income that is approximately what they would receive graduating college with a bachelor's degree. Their skill sets are valued, and the opportunities for employment can be abundant.

This chapter looks at how voc-tech school leaders, principals, and teachers are building relationships with businesses and employers. Through these connections, Massachusetts's young people establish a foundation for their futures, employers maintain their operations, and voc-tech education grows in importance in today's economy.

Introduction

When President Barack Obama selected just one high school at which to deliver a commencement address in 2014, he chose Worcester Technical High School, a uniquely successful district vocational school that owes much of its turnaround to the support of the Worcester business community.

In 2006, frustrated by a shortage of skilled workers in the Worcester area, local businesses donated time and money to build a new state-of-the-art campus to replace the aging trade school. Led by Edwin "Ted" Coghlin, chairman of Coghlin Electric in Worcester, and the Worcester Tech Board of Trustees, the fundraising included $3 million that was leveraged into a $30 million fund with state money to purchase the latest computer and information technology equipment.[16]

The new attention transformed the school. Worcester Tech's dropout rate fell from 4.7 percent in the 2003–2004 school year to 0.5 percent in the 2012–2013 school year. Not only was it well below the district average of 3.4 percent, but it was also the lowest among Worcester's seven high schools.[17]

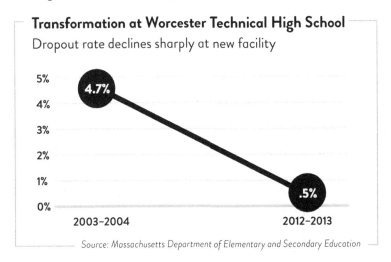

Transformation at Worcester Technical High School

Dropout rate declines sharply at new facility

Source: Massachusetts Department of Elementary and Secondary Education

In today's global economy, it is no longer possible for the United States to maintain its competitive advantage without tapping the potential of all its workers. Every student who chooses career training through a voc-tech school must be equipped with skills that are more sophisticated and advanced than those required in the industrial, manufacturing-based economy of 60 years ago.

No group understands this challenge more than our nation's manufacturers. To compete with global manufacturing giants like China, Germany, and Japan, they are constantly upgrading their physical plants, modernizing systems, and adopting new processes.

But their investments are often undermined by a lack of qualified workers to operate their production facilities. To offset that shortage, many:

- Collaborate with voc-tech schools to ensure their students are ready to work upon graduation
- Offer industry expertise as members of school advisory boards
- Donate sophisticated training equipment to school technical programs
- Team up on new technical programs and provide funds for startups

These collaborations have become vital across Massachusetts because many employers need new employees. Their businesses are expanding, and their current staffs are aging and retiring.

Manufacturers in Massachusetts account for 9.39 percent of the total output in the state, employing 7 percent of the workforce. Total output from manufacturing was $54.6 billion in 2019. In addition, there were an average of 236,000 manufacturing employees in Massachusetts in 2019, with an average annual compensation of nearly $104,000. (The latest available salary figures were for 2018.)

The skills needed for even the most conventional manufacturing jobs have changed dramatically as companies have incorporated new technology into their operations. Voc-tech schools have kept pace through new partnerships with local employers. Students who want to improve their employment prospects by obtaining concrete skills are choosing voc-tech programs and staying in school.

Voc-tech schools have also become part of the local economy through services provided by their students, including car repairs, cosmetology, and printing services. And restaurants at schools that offer a culinary arts program are open to the public, giving students an early start on learning the hospitality industry while being part of the local business community.

Today's Career Voc-Tech Schools

Voc-tech schools were once considered ideal for students who only planned to work in the trades and not continue to college. Not any longer. More than half of Massachusetts's voc-tech students go on to postsecondary education. About 20 percent more attend postsecondary training through continual learning and professional development related to their careers. Yet the schools still combine rigorous conceptual class work with practical application.

Majors in traditional trade programs such as carpentry, auto tech, health services, and cosmetology are offered along with robotics, biotechnology, advanced manufacturing, electronics, and engineering.

"When students in all our vocational schools cross the stage in June and accept their diplomas from high school, they can actually do something," said James J. Brosnan, superintendent of Charles H. McCann Technical School in North Adams. "They can be an electrician or a plumber or whatever. Other kids who cross the stage in high school can go on to the next level of education. Our students can do both."[18]

All Massachusetts's voc-tech high schools have advisory councils of 10 to 15 community members, including local tradespeople, practitioners, business owners, and managers.

Each career-technical program has its own dedicated team of advisors as well.

The role of the advisory council is to ensure that the school's programs are state of the art, to assist the superintendent in forecasting capital equipment needs, to maintain relevance of the equipment and curricula, and to help build stronger business-school partnerships.

Advisory councils are an important way for businesses to partner with voc-tech schools. They not only advise the shops, but act as their champions in the community. They offer co-ops and internships to students and, in many cases, offer employment after graduation.

- The Electrical program at Greater New Bedford Regional Vocational-Technical High School enjoys very strong ties with Holliston-based Wayne J. Griffin Electric, Inc. The company has provided many co-op opportunities to Greater New Bedford students over the years, including more than 65 full-time jobs. In addition, Griffin Electric has donated more than $70,000 in electrical supply equipment to the school.

- Greater New Bedford's Medical Assisting program has had a very long and valuable relationship with both Southcoast Hospitals Group and Steward Medical Group, who have long had a member on the voc-tech district's Advisory Committee. Steward Medical has offered placement and co-op opportunities to more than 500 of the school's students and hired more than 100 over the years. Southcoast Hospitals Group has donated thousands of dollars' worth of medical equipment to the school.

- At Old Colony Regional Vocational Technical High School in Rochester, Autocam Medical of Plymouth has participated in the co-op education program for more than 18 years and has employed more than 30 of the school's graduates. During that same period, they have supported Old Colony's Advanced Manufacturing Program with in-kind donations totaling $35,000.

Working together, voc-tech school officials and local employers have implemented a change in education delivery that has produced significantly lower dropout rates than comparable traditional high schools. The statewide dropout rate at regular/comprehensive high schools averaged 1.8 percent in 2018–2019 but was a mere 0.7 percent among the 41 voc-tech schools and averaged just 0.6 percent among regional voc-tech schools.[19]

In Springfield, Putnam Vocational Technical Academy's 0.4 percent dropout rate was well below the district average of 4.4 percent in the 2018–2019 school year. According to the United States Department of Education, federal involvement in voc-tech education, through the Perkins Act, helps students acquire challenging academic and technical skills and be prepared for high-skill, high-wage, or high-demand occupations in the twenty-first-century global economy.[20]

Support for Voc-Tech Education

Going forward, workers will increasingly require greater knowledge and more complex technological skills. State officials and the business community are both aware of the possibility that the shortage of skilled workers may worsen in the future and are working together with voc-tech schools to address the problem.

"Manufacturing has a great future," said Greg Bialecki, who served as the state's Secretary of Housing and Economic Development between 2009 and 2015. "They're looking for more people to hire, and we want to tell people it's a great career for [anyone] to consider."[21]

In 2010, the state's Economic Development Planning Council, the business community, academia, and the Legislature worked together to develop a strategic plan titled "Choosing to Compete in the 21st Century."

The plan's purpose was to create jobs and drive economic development across the Commonwealth. As part of that effort, and with the belief that manufacturing is an important part of the state's economic growth and stability, they created an Advanced Manufacturing Collaborative, whose mission is "to develop, coordinate and oversee the implementation of the state's advanced manufacturing strategy, with the goal of enhancing the competitiveness of the state's advanced manufacturing industry, for today and the future."

Several of the state's quasi-public agencies have played a significant role in assisting educational/business partnerships for economic development:

- Mass Development's *AMP it up!* campaign shows students, parents, guidance counselors, and teachers how advanced manufacturing careers can put them on the path to success. *AMP it up!* is for students who are builders and problem solvers. It can provide schools with resources, and students with the guidance they need for jobs in fields such as high-tech processing, factory automation, product development, and nanotechnology. They do this by helping students explore what it's like to work at an advanced manufacturing company. The program's motto? "No one dreams of working in a cubicle."

- The Commonwealth Corporation, another quasi-public organization, administers the Advanced Manufacturing, Technology & Hospitality Training Trust Fund on behalf of the Executive Office of Housing and Economic Development and the Executive Office of Labor and Workforce Development. The fund was established in 2014 to support training and education programs — especially in voc-tech settings — that address the workforce shortages of the advanced manufacturing, mechanical and technical skills, hospitality, and information technologies industries across the state.

- The Mass Life Sciences Center (MLSC) has been very supportive of voc-tech schools, especially those starting engineering programs. MLSC's Science, Technology, Engineering, and Math (STEM) Equipment and Supplies Grant Program:

  - Enables the purchase of equipment and supplies so Massachusetts schools can train students in life sciences technology and research
  - Addresses a capital funding gap for public and not-for-profit workforce training and educational institutions
  - Seeks to support the implementation of state STEM standards and to increase student achievement and student interest in STEM

To date, the STEM Equipment and Professional Development Grant Program has awarded more than $21.5 million to 240 different Massachusetts high schools and organizations and leveraged more than $4 million in matching funds from the life sciences industry.

- Massachusetts Manufacturing Extension Partnership (MassMEP) gave rise to a business-led and very active Massachusetts Advanced Center Workforce Collaborative (MACWIC). Founded in February 2012, MACWIC has over 225 member companies, representing more than 27,000 employees. The partnership's mission is to facilitate employer-led workforce training and initiatives, with the goals of preserving manufacturing knowledge and transferring that knowledge to the current and future workforce.

- In partnership with Worcester Polytechnic Institute (WPI), MACWIC has developed an Applied Manufacturing Technology Pathway Certification, which is recognized by employers. MACWIC and WPI also make a "Curriculum in a Box" and Learn CNC software available for free to any voc-tech school in Massachusetts that has a machine technology or manufacturing program. This program leads to additional MACWIC certifications.

  Through MACWIC, Siemens in April 2014 announced nearly $660 million of in-kind software grants for manufacturing programs at vocational high schools and institutions of higher learning. Massachusetts students in the recipient institutions now have access to the same Siemens product lifecycle management (PLM) software used in global manufacturing industries to design, develop, and manufacture a variety of sophisticated products.

- The Western Massachusetts Chapter of the National Tooling and Machining Association (WMNTMA), partners with voc-tech schools in the Pioneer Valley to help ensure graduates have the educational and technical competencies they need for employment in precision manufacturing. WMNTMA has developed the Regional Precision Manufacturing Technology Advisory, to provide strategic guidance and support to industry members on the Machine Tool Technology Program Advisory Committees (PAC's) at the technical/comprehensive high schools in the Pioneer Valley region. The technology advisory also helps them in collaborating with administrations and teachers in the successful operation of machine tool technology programs. This approach has led to a pooling of resources to fund career technical shops with the equipment required to properly train the employees they will need to keep their businesses strong.

Much of what these groups do is public relations for career voc-tech education. Even huge multinational corporations such as ExxonMobil have become players. In 2014, they launched a large, multimedia campaign, "Be an Engineer," to show young people how the many disciplines of engineering can be fun, exciting, and fulfilling.

The Value of Career Voc-Tech Education

Increasingly, Massachusetts families are seeing that voc-tech schools allow their children to simultaneously learn a trade and prepare for college. The rise in popularity has created waiting lists in the hundreds at many schools.

A closer look at how voc-tech schools develop graduates who are prepared both for careers and postsecondary education helps explain the growing popularity of these schools, which have produced graduating classes that have gone on to fill many of the most important jobs in the Commonwealth.

Case Study: Nashoba Valley Tech

Over the past 25 years, Nashoba Valley Technical High School in Westford grew from fewer than 100 graduates annually to a freshman class of nearly 200. There were 190 members in the freshman class in 2020–2021.

With the constant input of their active advisory committees, the school has closed programs that are no longer relevant to the local economy and has used the knowledge and generosity of their business community advisors to open new rigorous and relevant programs. Programs such as Horticulture, Upholstery, and Painting & Design were phased out, and TV, Media/Theater Arts, Programming & Web Development, and Engineering were opened.

Under the leadership of Superintendent Dr. Judith Klimkiewicz, ground was broken in July 2002 on a $25.5 million renovation and expansion project that added two wings to the existing building and completely renovated and updated all technical program areas, critical infrastructure, and academic classrooms.

One program that benefitted tremendously from the 2002 expansion was the Banking, Marketing & Retail program, which also developed a collaboration with the Lowell Five Cent Savings Bank. A full working bank branch was opened at Nashoba, staffed by a full-time bank employee who works side by side with career-tech students. In early 2014, a drive-up ATM on the school campus was opened, available to the public 24/7—a first for a public school in Massachusetts.

Nashoba Tech's most loyal sponsor has been Juniper Networks, whose headquarters are adjacent to the school. For many years, Juniper has been contributing computers, furnishings, and technical equipment, as well as funding, to its neighbor, and it is often Juniper that initiates the donations.

When Nashoba Tech built its state-of-the-art performing arts center and TV studio, it was Juniper that supplied the furniture for the theater; in return, they hold their yearly CEO meeting in the facility.

The TV studio's industry-standard Avid Media Composer software was supplied by an advisory committee member who was instrumental in getting the TV/Media program approved by the state.

The latest project at Nashoba Tech is the opening of their Engineering Academy, an interdisciplinary project that combines what would be, in other voc-tech schools, the drafting and electronics programs, with a fully state-certified engineering program.

The twist is that Nashoba's Engineering Academy is a school within a school. The 30 students in the academy are housed in one wing of the school. They rotate among a dedicated group of teachers who teach the engineering modules of the nationally respected engineering curriculum, Project Lead the Way (biotech, aerospace, geophysical, environmental, electrical, mechanical, architectural, civil, and telecommunications), as well as mathematics, science for engineering, and English. The students join the general population for social studies, Spanish, and music.

Nashoba Tech's interest in engineering began with their involvement—as it has with so many schools—in FIRST Robotics, sponsored by their business partners, Raytheon and NASA.

Maintaining a High Standard for Voc-Tech Education

By maintaining an open, fair, and careful application process for Chapter 74 schools, Massachusetts will continue to produce graduates who meet the high standards required and work ethic expected by the nation's employers, manufacturers, and institutions of higher learning.

In the fall of 2014, Dr. Michael F. Fitzpatrick, then Superintendent Director of Blackstone Valley Tech and a nationally recognized expert in career voc-tech education, addressed the Massachusetts Board of Elementary and Secondary Education on the reasons for the success of voc-tech in Massachusetts.

Dr. Fitzpatrick noted that multiple studies attribute voc-tech success to factors including professional development, an integrated and applied approach to academics, and teaming, both within schools and with the local and regional business communities.

Massachusetts's voc-tech systems use aggressive professional development that provides staff with relevant skills validated by industry, Dr. Fitzpatrick noted. Instruction needs to reflect that which industry demands and expects of today's workers.

Case Study: Westfield Technical Academy

Massachusetts's Pioneer Valley is home to an aviation cluster of airports, manufacturers, aircraft service centers, and flight schools.

In January 2014, several companies, including Gulfstream Aerospace, Rectrix Aviation, Embraer Executive Jet, Bombardier, and Mobius Works began working with state officials and school administrators at Westfield Vocational Technical High School to start the state's first high school aviation maintenance technology program.

Appropriately, the school was renamed Westfield Technical Academy the next year.

With industry giant Boeing forecasting that the global aviation industry will need a million new pilots and maintenance technicians during the next 20 years, their goal is to graduate more Westfield Tech students who are ready to join the workforce.

"They're interested in a lot of our programs," said Stefan Czaporowski, who served as Westfield's principal from 2012 to 2016 before his appointment to superintendent. "We know that there is a huge shortage, and they're willing to devote a lot of time to this because in the end it will benefit them."[22]

With this vision and tremendous support from business and industry, Westfield Technical Academy has the only Chapter 74 Aviation Maintenance Technology Program in Massachusetts.

Westfield Tech's program was certified by the Federal Aviation Administration (FAA) in August 2016. The Aviation Maintenance Technology Program utilizes both lecture and extensive hands-on training—both in shop and directly on aircraft—to meet the requirements of the federal government.

The program has 10 airplanes, two helicopters, two simulators, 38 state-of-the-art aircraft systems mockups, and equipment to train students in all the areas of aircraft maintenance.

Students in grades 9–12 who enter the program complete over 1,200 hours of classroom and shop over their four years of high school before being able to test for certification.

The students are required to complete 1,150 hours of required technical training per the FAA in general study (400 hours) and airframe study (750 hours). Westfield students exceed the requirement, averaging 1,226 hours of training—433 hours in general study and 793 hours in airframe study.

Instructors monitor each student through the entire program. They track all tests and evaluations to ensure that students maintain a sufficient grade point average. Instructors are required to annotate each hour of curriculum teaching. A master list is maintained for all students and progress reports are submitted to the FAA as required.

Faculty and guidance counselors assist students in achieving their academic/technical, workplace readiness, and personal/social potential. Placement upon graduation has been excellent. Every member of the June 2021 graduating class has gone on to an aviation postsecondary college, military service, or a job in the aviation industry.

Upon completion of the FAA-certified Aircraft Maintenance Technician program, students are eligible to test for their FAA license. Licensure allows students to go directly into the aviation maintenance industry as a certified technician. Additionally, colleges accept the license for credit toward a college degree.

None of this would be possible without exceptional support from industry. Key partners have included Gulfstream, Ross Aviation (Rectrix) of Westfield, Bombardier, based in Windsor Locks, Connecticut, and the Fly LUGU (Look-up Go-up) Flight School, also in Westfield.

In addition, the 25-member Aviation Advisory Board, including dedicated community members who have an interest in aviation and/or education, plays a vital role in supporting the program.

The exceptional success of the program at Westfield Tech has motivated three additional Massachusetts voc-tech schools to begin feasibility studies for the development of Chapter 74 Aviation Maintenance Technology Programs.

Case Study: McCann Technical School

The Route 128 belt in eastern Massachusetts is internationally known as a high-technology hub, but at the western end of the state, Berkshire County has its own industrial claim. The region has often been called the "plastics research technology center of the nation" because of the high concentration of plastics manufacturers among the Berkshire Hills. Berkshire County hosts more plastics firms than any other county in the nation, with SABIC Innovative Plastics (formerly GE Plastics) as a core.

Since its opening in 1962, students graduating from the Charles H. McCann Technical School in North Adams have provided a steady source of employees for local industries. Still, the rapid change in technology used by those manufacturers has created a challenge to find skilled labor as their businesses expand.

Two major software makers who sell to the smaller manufacturers of Berkshire County have the same concern. In 2013, Cimatron and Siemens PLM Software donated millions of dollars' worth of specialized software to McCann. The gifts enable McCann students to use the same technology in their classrooms that companies throughout Berkshire County and around the globe are using each day to design products.

The donation represents the sort of collaboration that private industry and voc-tech schools can make to train students for jobs and bolster the local economy by helping manufacturers to compete.

"In western Massachusetts we have a lot of the niche manufacturers that make precision pieces," said James J. Brosnan, superintendent at McCann. "These are smaller companies that employ 25 to 40 people and who have a worldwide market of very sophisticated pieces. They need a very well-educated workforce. The companies know that for 50 years they've been dealing with McCann, and they've gotten 50 years of McCann workers and they can keep replacing them because we keep producing them."[23]

McCann connects with local manufacturers through its co-op program and through their representatives on the school's 22-member vocational advisory committee. Brosnan said about 35 to 40 companies participate in the co-op program, which is open to qualified students during the second half of their junior year and during their senior year.

In the fall of 2014, 32 McCann students were working with companies on co-op. McCann also connects with companies through Project Lead the Way, a national science, technology, engineering, and math program that prepares students for high-tech careers.

Students at McCann create tech projects that are viewed by professionals in the field. The students earn articulation credits to colleges such as Worcester Polytechnic Institute and Rochester Institute of Technology.

In fact, McCann's participation in Project Lead the Way prompted Siemens to contact the school about donating its software. Siemens NX software was awarded to McCann through Siemens' "GO PLM" grant program. In addition to using the software in class, school officials plan to host a "manufacturing summer camp" to introduce students in the fifth, sixth, and seventh grades to modern manufacturing.

The Cimatron donation came about after the vice president of engineering at Cimatron visited a local business that uses his company's software and learned that many of the employees there were McCann graduates. Intrigued, he visited the school and offered to donate 25 licenses of the company's CimatronE software.

Computer-aided design students use it to design injection molds. Machine technology students use it to produce parts and components to given specifications. It also allows students to use an advanced machining simulation before operating the CNC equipment on the shop floor.

"Because we have the equipment and latest software, having a co-op student from McCann is very desirable," said Brosnan. "That 17-year-old or 18-year-old senior is able to bring the latest techniques in, and on a number of occasions they have helped train the workforce. Employees who are 40 or 50 years old might receive training from them. We think that's terrific because it helps with the student's maturation process."

The challenge for the manufacturing sector today is to make it attractive to younger workers. Brosnan points out that it is not the factory of old, where someone stands at the same machine all day while someone else stands at another machine. Today, with computer numerical code manufacturing centers, one person is responsible for multiple machines, inputting the process, making sure the product is there, and making program changes.

"So, instead of having four or five people on a hand machine, you have one person that has to have software programing knowledge for that equipment, as well as the product and the metallurgy and more," Brosnan said.

Conclusions and Recommendations

With the more sophisticated demands of the new economy in mind, curriculum in the voc-tech setting must be viewed as an active process which promotes vigorous, thought-provoking, facilitating, and individual assessment activities to develop each student's potential as a learner.

Students must be given the opportunity to acquire an understanding of the technical application of the STEM processes essential to their given trade areas and to improve their total skills if they are to reach their individual potential in the new workplace.

The Massachusetts model of voc-tech education—with its alternating academic and technical shop weeks—is well suited for authentic learning in STEM; and science, math, and engineering processes are integrated in every career technical shop, as well as each academic classroom.

This model should be protected, replicated, and made available to the one-third of Massachusetts cities and towns that do not belong to a regional voc-tech district. Additionally, this will give more regional employers the chance to help shape and make more relevant the career-technical curricula being taught to prospective employees. Moreover, it will create additional opportunities for industry to work with the next generation to ensure that they are graduating as skilled members of society.

- To supply the skilled employees that Massachusetts's industries need, continued administrative and legislative funding support for grants and training programs for voc-tech schools is an economic imperative. Manufacturing and business groups should grow their advisory roles into public-private partnerships that will strengthen the high-skills pipeline.

- A key element in making voc-tech education available to all students who would benefit from it—and thereby training the workforce today's manufacturers are looking for—is to change any district policies that make voc-tech education a random or neighborhood choice among all other high schools in a district. Data show that when a student has chosen voc-tech education, rather than having had it imposed, the academic and professional results can be remarkable.

- Along with making urban voc-tech schools into schools of choice, district-run voc-tech administrations should be given the same autonomy over budget and staffing that is enjoyed by regional voc-tech officials. Additionally, the Chapter 74 and Perkins funding that is granted to urban districts to support vocational programming should be funneled directly to the schools that host those programs, rather than being distributed throughout the district for general education.

■ ■ ■

Alison L. Fraser is an education policy, research, and strategy consultant and president of Practical Policy. Previously, she was an administrator at Blackstone Valley Tech and director of policy and advocacy at Mass Insight Education, where she directed the Great Schools Campaign and development of No Excuses for Failing Schools and Excellence in Math and Science Goals. An expert in standards-based curriculum, Fraser has coordinated activities and programs for the Coalition for Higher Standards and led research in standards-based reform.

William Donovan is a former staff writer with the Providence Journal in Rhode Island, where he wrote about business and government. He has taught business journalism in the graduate programs at Boston University and Northeastern University. He received his undergraduate degree from Boston College and his master's degree in Journalism from American University in Washington, D.C.

Chapter 3

Hands-On Achievement: Why Massachusetts's Vocational-Technical Schools Have Low Dropout Rates

by Alison L. Fraser with William Donovan

More than one million students drop out of high school in the United States each year, setting them on courses of lost income, diminished health, and increased odds of incarceration.[24] Collectively, their decisions cost the nation hundreds of billions of dollars in lost revenue, lower economic activity, and increased need for social services.[25]

It is an epidemic in education that has been treated with an array of remedies at the federal, state, and local levels. But just as the mysteries of some physical diseases have stymied a cure, the myriad causes of students leaving school without a high school diploma—lack of interest, the need to support themselves and family, failing grades, family problems—have prevented educators and policy makers from solving the dropout crisis.

Gains have been made, however. Across the country, studies have found that career voc-tech education appeals to students across the spectrum, including those in danger of not earning a high school diploma. By demonstrating the practical uses of abstract concepts, voc-tech education answers the ancient teenage lament: "Why am I learning this?"

In Massachusetts, where an average of 6,400 high school students have dropped out of school annually over each of the past 10 years,[26] the state's voc-tech network has been particularly effective at keeping students in school.

The statewide dropout rate at regular/comprehensive high schools averaged 1.8 percent in 2018–2019 but was only 0.7 percent among the 41 voc-tech schools and averaged a mere 0.6 percent among regional voc-tech schools.[27]

Superintendents and principals say a mix of academic choice, applied learning, intense mentor relationships, and high expectations has kept their dropout counts down, despite generally having student populations that have larger percentages of special needs students than the state high school average.

"Today there is writing across the curriculum in every vocational program," said David Ferreira, former executive director of the Massachusetts Association of Vocational Administrators (MAVA). "We're building academic competencies and using the training in the vocational area as the way to get students engaged and excited."[28]

The 1906 founding document for voc-tech education in Massachusetts recognized the necessity for both technical knowledge and skills to address the needs of industry and the individual. This document provided the blueprint for the country to deal with increasing industrial technology and the ineffectiveness of public education in retaining its students.[29]

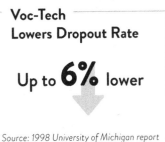

Voc-Tech Lowers Dropout Rate

Up to **6%** lower

Source: 1998 University of Michigan report

During the past 15 years, studies have noted voc-tech's success in discouraging students from leaving school before graduation. A 1998 report by the University of Michigan found that high-risk students are eight to 10 times less likely to drop out in the 11th and 12th grades if they enroll in a career technical education program instead of a general program.

The report also stated that a quality career voc-tech education could lower a school's dropout rate by as much as 6 percent. Importantly, it also found that voc-tech students are less likely than students at a comprehensive high school to fail a course or to be absent.[30]

In 2005, the National Research Center for Career and Technical Education reported that students entering high school at a typical or younger age had a decreased risk of dropping out as they added voc-tech courses to their curriculum.

The report suggests that a combination of voc-tech education and academic courses can lower the dropout rate as students are exposed to a broader range of experiences and can more easily envision careers in their futures.[31]

In a 2007 brief, the Association for Career and Technical Advancement cited five potential benefits of career and technical education for at-risk students.[32] They included:

- Enhancement of students' motivation and academic achievement
- Increased personal and social competence related to work in general
- A broad understanding of an occupation or industry
- Career exploration and planning
- Acquisition of knowledge or skills related to employment in particular occupations or more generic work competencies

How Voc-Tech Education Works

At career voc-tech schools, students receive in-depth training in majors such as electronics, construction, medical assisting, or biotechnology.

Typically, they spend the first half of their freshman year exploring up to 10 career and technical majors offered at their school. They then select the ones that most interest them and, through a rubric system, are matched with a voc-tech laboratory, or shop.

Over the next three-and-a-half years, students proceed on

an alternating schedule. One full week is spent in shop focusing on their chosen vocation, the next week in traditional academic classes. This is a proven approach that keeps students absorbed in school by connecting abstract classroom concepts with hands-on practical applications.

"Vocational education provides us the opportunity to teach academic skills, math and science in particular, in a real-life situation," said MAVA's Ferreira. "To put up rafters on the roof of a house, for example, utilizes fundamentals of trigonometry. They see the relationship between the academic and the physical skills needed to build a house and put a roof on."[33]

The alternating schedule and concentrated major mean students work closely with the same teachers for over three-and-a-half years. Teachers at voc-tech schools must be licensed by the Massachusetts Department of Elementary and Secondary Education (DESE). Additionally, they are required to have three to five years of professional experience in the field in which they are licensed.

Unlike teachers at comprehensive high schools, whose contact with students is limited to a class period and perhaps after-school programs, voc-tech teachers are with 10 to 15 students all day every other week. These adults develop mentoring roles and are alert to subtle changes that may signal the beginning of an issue that could cause a student to drop out of school.

"The instructors are our eyes and ears," said Sheila Harrity, former principal of Worcester Technical High School and now superintendent at Montachusett Regional Vocational Technical High School. "When a student goes into crisis or has a problem, they are the ones who hear of it firsthand and are able to assist or redirect the student."[34]

Voc-tech school officials say their attendance expectations of students play a role in their low dropout levels. Students learn their skills through repetition that can only be practiced at school. Students know that without putting in their "time on task" in school they'll be ill prepared when they work with an employer.

In a 2006 survey, Massachusetts industry professionals generally agreed that voc-tech graduates are better prepared for post-high school life than most college preparatory graduates, not only because of the workplace skills they have acquired but also because of the work ethic they have developed.[35]

"You need to engage and involve children in their education, particularly at the high school level," said Charles Lyons, retired superintendent of Shawsheen Valley Technical High School in Billerica. "If you do that and get them to come to school, you have incredible results."[36]

Inside the Dropout Numbers

The Massachusetts DESE defines dropouts as "those students who dropped out of school between July 1 and June 30 of a given year and who did not return to school, graduate, or receive a GED by the following October 1."

The annual dropout rate is calculated by dividing the number of students who drop out over a one-year period by the October 1 grades 9–12 enrollment, multiplied by 100.[37]

Prior to the 1992–1993 school year, DESE reported an unadjusted dropout rate, which did not account for students who left school but returned by the following October 1. Until the 1994–1995 school year, DESE published an unadjusted rate and an adjusted rate developed by the U.S. Department of Education. The adjusted rate partially accounted for those returning students.

Beginning in the 1995–1996 school year, DESE reported only an adjusted rate. That meant its annual figures would no longer be comparable to data for years prior to 1993.

An additional reporting change came in 2002–2003, when, for the first time, the dropout rate was based on student-level data submitted by districts through the Student Information Management System (SIMS), "a student-level data collection system that allows the Department to collect and analyze more accurate and comprehensive information (and), to meet federal and state reporting requirements."[38]

Prior to the 2001–2002 school year, dropout figures had been reported by districts in aggregate form in the Year-End School Indicator Report. Another significant change occurred in the 2005–2006 school year, when DESE began to cross-reference SIMS data with the General Educational Development (GED) Testing Service database.

This enabled DESE more accurately to track students who drop out of high school but subsequently earn a GED, thereby decreasing the number of students considered dropouts in the final count.

Since the 1995–1996 school year, when the dropout rate for both voc-tech schools and regular/comprehensive high schools was 3.4 percent, voc-tech schools have consistently posted dropout rates that are at least a full percentage point lower than regular high schools.

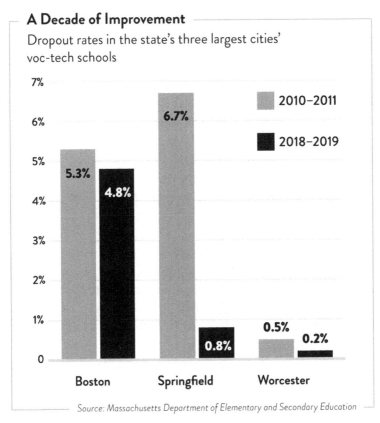

A Decade of Improvement

Dropout rates in the state's three largest cities' voc-tech schools

- 2010–2011
- 2018–2019

Boston: 5.3% / 4.8%
Springfield: 6.7% / 0.8%
Worcester: 0.5% / 0.2%

Source: Massachusetts Department of Elementary and Secondary Education

While the average dropout rate for comprehensive high schools was 2.8 percent in the 2010–2011 school year, among voc-tech schools the rate ranged from zero to a high of 2.1 percent among regional voc-tech schools.

Essex Agricultural and Technical High School in the Hathorne section of Danvers and North Shore Technical High School in Middleton — two schools merged in 2014 to form Essex Technical High School — had zero dropouts in the 2010–2011 school year.

In that same year, Whittier Regional Vocational Technical High School in Haverhill, with an enrollment of 1,251 students, had just two dropouts. Shawsheen Valley Technical High School, with an enrollment of 1,324 students, had only three dropouts.

These exemplary numbers were posted by regional voc-tech schools while working with more at-risk students than are present in most comprehensive high schools.

Though the average percentage of special needs students in Massachusetts is 18.7 percent, the average percentage of students with special needs in regional voc-tech schools is 22.5 percent. Five schools have greater than 30 percent of their students on IEPs, ranging up to 44.1 percent special needs students at Minuteman Regional Vocational Technical High School in Lexington.

Still, the graduation rate of special needs students at vocational schools is almost 20 percentage points higher, with 73.9 percent of students with disabilities graduating.

There is a difference in the dropout rates of the 26 regional voc-tech schools in the Commonwealth vis-à-vis the nine urban, district-run voc-tech schools.

Regional voc-tech schools averaged a remarkable 0.6 percent dropout rate in 2018–2019, while the rate for city-run voc-tech schools was 4.4 percent. That city school rate was the lowest posted in the past 17 years, and figures from voc-tech schools across the state reflect an overall trend toward much lower dropout rates than in the past.

Holyoke High School's Dean Campus had a dropout rate of 3.6 percent in 2018–2019 while the Center for Technical

Education Innovation in Leominster had a rate of 1.8 percent.

In the 2018–2019 school year, Roger L. Putnam Vocational Technical Academy in Springfield recorded a 0.8 percent rate and Lynn Vocational Technical Institute a 0.6 percent rate.

Other schools are also driving their numbers down. The dropout rate for Madison Park Technical Vocational High School in Boston plunged from 9.4 percent in 2006–2007 to 5.3 percent in 2010–2011, and went still lower, to just 4.8 percent, in 2018–2019.

Demographics are one reason for the difference in dropout rates between regional and urban voc-tech schools. One city principal said the dropout rates in cities can be higher than in the suburbs because there is a larger immigrant population and the possibility of more students leaving school to return to their native lands. Ferreira also thinks that some cities have been slower to recognize the new role that voc-tech schools are playing.

"Some of it has to do with the nature of being a city school as opposed to being in a regional school district, and the way a city might look upon the role of the vocational school," Ferreira said. "I think there has been a slower change to recognize that it is no longer a place to put kids who are not pursuing college or who tend toward more physical labor."[39]

Though every voc-tech school is engaging its students through applied learning—combining classroom lessons with practical experience—each school is different, and their stories are instructional. The experiences of four schools in achieving low dropout rates can be useful to other school administrators and principals.

Blackstone Valley Regional Vocational Technical High School

Blackstone Valley Tech serves 13 municipalities in south-central Massachusetts, encompassing the towns of the Blackstone Valley, which is widely accepted as the birthplace of the American Industrial Revolution. These former mill towns have a unique identity, which they preserve while moving into the twenty-first century and attracting new and cutting-edge industries and technologies that will keep younger generations employed in the area.

Valley Tech has long played a central role in this transformation, partnering with area businesses to identify workforce needs that its students can meet.

The population of these communities is solidly middle class. For example, the percentage of students receiving free or reduced-price lunch is only 19 percent. The students served by Valley Tech are often left out of education reform equations, yet these students—often average to lower-than-average academically—respond to very high expectations by posting above-average achievement and demonstrating high rates of college and career readiness and success.

With a dropout rate of just 0.3 percent, a graduation rate of 98.2 percent (compared to the state's 83.4 percent), a truancy rate of 0 percent, and 100 percent of students graduating with a competency determination for the past 10 years, Valley Tech is clearly a model of education reform that deserves replication.

Anthony Steele II, the Assistant Superintendent-Director/ Principal at Valley Tech, said students' feeling that voc-tech education is more relevant to them is the key to low dropout rates.[40]

According to Steele, students who are more academically inclined appreciate the relevance of integrating core academic concepts into shop curricula. For students who appreciate the incentive of being fully prepared to get a job upon graduation, the real-life reward of being employable is extremely relevant.

"We can't lose sight of the kids who understand the vocational value of being at Valley Tech," Steele said. "It's apparent in the number of students who will meet any shop or academic benchmark necessary to get the privilege of going out on a co-op job in their area of study."

The root of Valley Tech's success is integration. The district has accepted with enthusiasm the challenge presented at the local, state, and national levels to increase student achievement by refining innovative teaching methods and instructional strategies.

Using a comprehensive team approach, Valley Tech's faculty have organized model curricular and instructional practices into a single integrated high school experience which combines academic and career/technical learning, promotes opportunities for students, and creates workforce solutions for employers.

Integration has been Valley Tech's philosophy since before education reform in 1993, but they knew they could not achieve the desired academic and vocational successes without more time on learning.

Therefore, over time, the school year was lengthened to 195 days — the longest public school year in the state. Common sense would point toward students rebelling against this extra time in school, but conversely, for the entering freshman class in 2012, there were 800 applicants for the 300 available spaces. The admissions process is meticulously blind and accepts a true cross-section of the sending districts.

At Valley Tech, academic teachers routinely coordinate lesson plans with their voc-tech colleagues, using topics, themes, and subject matter related to students' career fields to reinforce academic concepts and ideas.

Additionally, all students take year-long courses on the employability, technology competency, and management and entrepreneurship strands of the voc-tech frameworks. These courses, run by academic staff in conjunction with school counseling staff during the academic week, reinforce, integrate, and personalize instruction over each student's four-year high school experience.

Even with the longer year, attendance rates at Valley Tech, as at the other regional voc-tech schools, are significantly higher than statewide averages, and higher attendance rates translate into lower dropout rates.

"Students come to our schools more regularly," Steele said, "because if they're not comfortable in a paper-and-pencil environment and are more inclined to be at ease with hands-on learning, it's easier for them to tolerate the voc-tech model. Despite their best intentions with conventional teaching and learning methodologies, they know that they will be able to express their growth and knowledge differently every other week."

At Valley Tech, each shop is equipped with assistive technology, and has teaching assistants assigned to it, to support students with IEPs. More significantly, each student is regularly assessed to determine whether he or she is reaching benchmarks determined by the state frameworks in a timely manner; if not, that student is given customized supports to achieve acceptable skill levels.

"Similar to a five-star restaurant where efficient service is linked with quality cuisine and artful presentation, effective curricular integration requires creative teaching methodology blended with relevant competencies," said former longtime Valley Tech Superintendent Dr. Michael Fitzpatrick.

The Valley Tech faculty and administration, believing that surprises can lead to frustration and students giving up, make sure that students always know where they stand academically and vocationally.

There is an iParent system in place, whereby parents or guardians can track student assignments and progress. Furthermore, every student who is absent for three days or more — whether for illness, bereavement, suspension, or any other reason — has a reentry meeting. That meeting is held immediately upon the student's return. Guidance, nursing staff, the dean of students, and teaching staff plan makeup work to guarantee a smooth reintegration with the school community.

Nashoba Valley Technical High School

While traditional high schools draw their students from the city or town in which they are located, often with a large population, students at regional voc-tech schools come from multiple communities.

However, some voc-tech schools lack a large anchor community that provides the bulk of their students, making it more challenging to recruit students. Such is the case for Nashoba Valley Technical High School in Westford, a regional school that has maintained a low dropout rate and raised enrollment by revamping its course offerings to appeal to its district communities.

Since the 2005–2006 school year, Nashoba has had an average annual dropout rate of just 0.6 percent, including 0 percent in 2008–2009 and 0.4 percent in 2018–2019.

The towns in the Nashoba district—Ayer, Chelmsford, Groton, Littleton, Pepperell, Shirley, Townsend, and Westford—collectively have the second-highest median income of all regional voc-tech districts in the state, according to Dr. Judith Klimkiewicz, Nashoba's former superintendent.[41]

Since the mid-1990s, enrollment has grown from 300 students to more than 700, largely because the school revised curriculum to reflect the interests of the district communities and retain students once they arrived.

"We had to do things differently," Klimkiewicz said. "We had to address programs that were more attractive to the communities we serve. We got rid of welding, painting, and decorating, and brought in pre-engineering, robotics, and dental assisting."

When Klimkiewicz became superintendent, she began a six-year plan of closing programs that had poor enrollment or minimal prospects for serving the community. The district used U.S. Department of Labor data, a review of postsecondary programs, and surveys of local employers to revamp offerings in line with their member communities' needs.

"Many of our towns feel every one of their students should go to Harvard," Klimkiewicz said. "They're just not going off to a regular college, they're going off to an Ivy League school. We had to improve and do a lot of things that other schools did not need to do."

The district emphasizes the importance of student attendance. Every child absent from school receives a call from the dean of students. After three unexcused absences in a trimester, the student fails.

Every achievement a student can earn, including Student of the Month, Leadership Club, and participation in co-op or internships, is based on good attendance.

"They can't get their certification for some of the programs without their hours," Klimkiewicz said. "They can't get their cosmetology license, their electrical license, their plumbing license, or their certified nursing assistant license without those hours committed."

After the 2010–2011 school year, 82 percent of graduates went off to postsecondary training, including two- and four-year colleges. Klimkiewicz said a large percentage of those college-bound students are special education students, who make up over 30 percent of the student population at Nashoba.

Klimkiewicz also said about two dozen students have graduated with a high school diploma and an associate degree through the school's dual-enrollment program.

Shawsheen Valley Technical High School

Simple math explains why Shawsheen Valley Technical High School has an exceptionally low dropout rate: Attendance equals graduation. Average daily attendance at Shawsheen rose from 93.8 percent in 2004 to 97 percent in the 2010–2011 school year, according to Superintendent Charles Lyons, who led the district from 1986 through 2020 and was succeeded by Bradford L. Jackson.[42]

During the same period, the school's annual dropout rate averaged 0.7 percent, including a mere 0.2 percent in 2010–2011.[43]

"The only way kids learn is to go to school and provide them with exceptional teachers and resources," said Lyons. "Our students are in school, we have exceptional teachers, and the students graduate on time."

Shawsheen administrators and teachers emphasize attendance in several ways:

- The superintendent receives a report on each Shawsheen student whose attendance dips below 90 percent and a corrective action plan is created to raise that figure.
- The school's guidance counselors work with students to modify their behavior and improve their attendance.
- A social worker in the office of the dean of students calls students when they miss school.

These efforts have produced a dropout rate that is well below the 1.2 percent average combined rate of the public high schools in the five towns within the Shawsheen district—Bedford, Billerica, Burlington, Tewksbury, and Wilmington.

Once students are at school they need to be engaged. Lyons believes vocational education is effective for students who are right-brain learners—those who understand things more easily through experimentation—rather than left-brain learners who advance through memorization.

Those right-brain learners struggle to grasp concepts on a chalkboard in regular high schools, but they succeed in voc-tech schools through applied learning.

"In traditional high schools, unless you're a really talented kid, they can bore the heck out of you," said Lyons. "These kids are doing 75 text messages a day. Then they walk into high school and the teacher says take out your paper and pencil and let's take notes. That's boring.

"If a student says he wants to be a plumber, we say OK, but in order to be a plumber who makes a decent living, you're going to have to be able to do algebraic functions," Lyons added. "We tell them they'll need to have high communication skills to be an effective marketer and expand their business opportunities. They understand there's a relevance to what they're doing in school and why they're being asked to excel academically as well as in their vocation."

At Shawsheen, some of those right-brain students are making connections in a $4.5 million, 14,500-square-foot life science wing that opened in September 2011. There, the school has enhanced its existing health care programs by expanding training for health care technicians, medical and laboratory technicians, and dental assisting technicians.

At Shawsheen, the change in life sciences career-tech programs is the result of a constant review of school offerings to ensure that students are in programs that fit with job opportunities upon graduation or with college and career paths with promising employment opportunities.

Among the people conducting the regular program assessments are local business owners and managers, many of whom are involved in Shawsheen's co-op program.

In the 2011–2012 school year, Lyons said, 170 of the 321 seniors were working with 155 local employers, many of them small businesses of fewer than 10 employees.

As with all regional voc-tech schools, each of Shawsheen's technology and vocational programs has an advisory council of 10 to 15 community members, including local business managers. The role of each group is to ensure that the school's programs are state-of-the-art, assist the superintendent in forecasting capital equipment needs to maintain the relevancy of programs offered by the voc-tech school, and help the students get jobs.

"If we're going to invite employers in to help us with the first two things, then we need their help in securing employment for our students," said Lyons.

Worcester Technical High School

When students at Worcester Technical High School enter the cafeteria each day, they see a banner on the wall that has their handprint and signature, as well as those of their classmates. It also has a message stating their intention to graduate from high school.

"It's a promissory note to themselves and their classmates that they will graduate in four years," said Sheila Harrity, former principal of the school. "Every day at lunch they see their handprint. Our dropout rate is low because of that commitment."[44]

In schools across the country, the dropout rate is often higher among schools located in urban areas where the problems of gang violence, poverty, and family dynamics can derail students' attempts to graduate from high school.

Yet in Worcester, the state's second largest city, Worcester Tech is defying the odds. In the 2010–2011 school year, Worcester Tech's dropout rate was just 0.5 percent, well under the statewide average of 2.7 percent and the 0.9 percent dropout rate for all voc-tech schools in the Commonwealth. Among its sister urban district-controlled voc-tech schools, whose average dropout rate was 4.4 percent in 2010–2011, Worcester Tech had the lowest rate.

Perhaps more impressive is how Worcester Tech compares with schools in its own backyard. The district-wide dropout rate among the seven high schools in Worcester was 3.7 percent in 2010–2011, and Worcester Tech, with its 1,400 students, has the largest enrollment in the city.

Certainly, the $90 million, 400,000-square-foot facility that Worcester Tech opened in 2006 makes for a more attractive environment than older schools. But Worcester Tech's low dropout rate and 95.8 percent graduation rate are a marked turnaround from where the school was a decade before that.

Paired with the new facility was a new educational attitude that gave Worcester Tech the autonomy it needed to operate on its own, as a separate career voc-tech entity, and not "just another Worcester high school."

"We needed to address the rigor of the academics connected to the technical program," said Harrity. "We certainly had strength in the technical program, and we had state-of-the-art technology and equipment to support that, but we needed the integrated approach that really made student education relevant."

Worcester Tech began incorporating more Advanced Placement courses into its four small learning communities: Alden Design & Engineering, Coghlin Construction Technology, Information Technology & Business Services, and Allied Health & Human Services academies.

In addition, Worcester Tech was approved as a Massachusetts Math + Science Initiative (MMSI) school, a program to increase participation in AP courses among underserved populations, with a pledge to increase AP offerings in science, technology, engineering, and math. Advanced Placement enrollment was up 93 percent in the 2010–2011 school year compared to the prior year.

The more challenging courses are combined with equally challenging technical programs, anchored by teachers whom Harrity called "masters of their trade." She said that in addition to having the required state teaching certifications, instructors at Worcester Tech are on top of industry trends to ensure that students become "career and culture ready."

Recommendations

Give district-run career voc-tech schools more autonomy

In urban school districts, where low-income and immigrant populations are higher than in suburban areas, the dropout rate is also higher. Yet in the state's largest cities, the dropout rates of the voc-tech schools are below district averages and often among the lowest in a given city. Those trends have continued to improve over the last decade, according to dropout figures from 2018–2019, the latest made available by the state.

- In Boston, Madison Park Vocational Technical High School — among the city's six largest schools with a population of more than 800 students—had a 4.8 percent dropout rate in 2018–2019, slightly higher than the district average of 4.4 percent.

- In Springfield, Roger L. Putnam Vocational Technical Academy's 0.8 percent dropout rate was well below the district average of 4.4 percent.

- Worcester Technical High School's 0.2 percent dropout rate for 2018–2019 was not only lower than the district average of 2.6 percent, but it was also the lowest rate among the city's high schools.

Voc-tech education can provide low-income and immigrant students with job-ready skills faster than a comprehensive high school can do so. The small learning environments and the close relationships that vocational teachers develop with their students are ideal for urban schools, where teenagers are at a higher risk of dropping out.

As detailed in this chapter and in DESE data, when voc-tech schools and programs enjoy autonomy, they are significantly more successful — especially at retaining students — than voc-tech schools and programs that are run as part of a large district.

Generally, district-run voc-tech schools do not have the independence and self-governance needed to set their own budgets, write their own integrated curriculum, and create the specialized faculty and staffs needed to realize the successes commonly enjoyed by their autonomous regional peer organizations, which have their own superintendents, practices, schedules, and district policies.

A blue-ribbon panel created in 2012 to study Boston's in-district voc-tech school, Madison Park, came to the same conclusion:

"The Review Team believes that Madison Park needs more flexibility. This core principle has already been recognized around the Commonwealth, since most of the regional vocational technical high schools function independently of the districts they serve. They have the freedom to set policies and procedures appropriate for a vocational technical high school, and to establish conditions that recognize the unique responsibilities and needs of their students, their teachers and their programs. In contrast, Madison Park currently operates as other comprehensive Boston high schools."[45]

We believe that this holds true for all in-district voc-tech high schools that are not given the freedom to operate up to the vocational and academic standards required to create a strong program.

Create more vocational-technical schools

The success of voc-tech education in Massachusetts has created more interest among families. Waiting lists have developed at most schools, prompting at least one state legislator to propose a change in admissions policies at voc-tech schools, which place a high value on behavior, because of the state-of-the-art equipment and safety issues involved at voc-tech schools.

But such a change, essentially lowering admissions standards for voc-tech schools, would be a backward step. It suggests that voc-tech schools should be places to channel students of whom less is expected. In fact, in today's competitive job market, employers in the trades are looking for well-educated, qualified workers just as much as companies in white-collar sectors.

Massachusetts citizens would benefit from statewide leadership to open additional regional voc-tech schools to address the growing demand for career-technical education.

Reinvest in vocational-technical schools

In the 1960s, policy makers made voc-tech schools ready for the twentieth century. Now, at the dawn of the third decade of the twenty-first century, some of the state's voc-tech schools are 60 years old. It's time to reinvest in them again.

In April 2012, the administration of Governor Deval Patrick filed a supplemental capital bond bill to secure $5 million in funding over five years to help vocational schools upgrade laboratories and shop equipment.

The Patrick Administration's approach was replaced under Governor Charlie Baker with the Massachusetts Workforce Skills Cabinet, which aligns the Executive Offices of Education, Labor and Workforce Development, and Housing and Economic Development around a comprehensive economic growth agenda.

Created by executive order, the Cabinet is charged with creating and implementing a strategy to ensure that individuals can develop and continuously improve their skills and knowledge to meet the varying hiring needs of employers across the Commonwealth.

To date, the Baker Administration has awarded more than $30 million in Workforce Skills Capital Grants to Chapter 74 vocational technical and agricultural schools serving 54,300 students.

Support an awareness campaign about vocational-technical education

The administration and the DESE should work with practitioners to support a customized public relations campaign to bring attention to the successes of voc-tech schools in the Commonwealth.

For many people, the false impression persists that these schools are for students who aren't serious, are discipline problems, or are not college material. Yet, for many families, the choice of attending a career voc-tech school could be ideal for a student who is interested in learning to apply specific skills, while also moving on to postsecondary education.

Such a program could focus on the low dropout rates, internship opportunities, postgraduation job placements, and percentage of students who are accepted to two- or four-year colleges.

■ ■ ■

Alison L. Fraser is an education policy, research, and strategy consultant and president of Practical Policy. Previously, she was an administrator at Blackstone Valley Tech and director of policy and advocacy at Mass Insight Education, where she directed the Great Schools Campaign and development of No Excuses for Failing Schools and Excellence in Math and Science Goals. An expert in standards-based curriculum, Fraser has coordinated activities and programs for the Coalition for Higher Standards and led research in standards-based reform.

William Donovan is a former staff writer with the Providence Journal in Rhode Island, where he wrote about business and government. He has taught business journalism in the graduate programs at Boston University and Northeastern University. He received his undergraduate degree from Boston College and his master's degree in Journalism from American University in Washington, D.C.

Chapter 4

The Healing Hand: Modeling Catholic Medical Vocational-Technical Schooling

by Alison L. Fraser and William Donovan

Historically, Catholic college preparatory and career vocational-technical schools have had contrasting approaches to secondary school education. Catholic schools have provided classical liberal arts education, including religious instruction, with emphasis on the spiritual and intellectual potential of every student and an eye toward higher education. Voc-tech programs have been for kids who weren't "college material," weren't plunging into Shakespeare or the arts, and who intended to find a career in the trades.

In the Archdiocese of Boston today, many Catholic high schools are struggling with enrollment declines. Meanwhile, public voc-tech schools in Massachusetts are thriving, some with long waiting lists.

The ironic outcome is that Catholic school leaders are starting to see voc-tech education as a way to stop their enrollment slide — although not by opening multi-discipline voc-tech schools or adding a costly robotics or metal fabrication course. Rather, they are considering a medical arts program, where the barriers to entry are lower and opportunities are abundant.

But questions persist: Is it affordable? Is it manageable? Is it Catholic?

Catholic schools are successful runways for college-bound students. According to the Archdiocese of Boston, Catholic high school students had an average SAT score of 1605 in 2020, higher than Massachusetts (1119) and national (1051) averages. Among Archdiocese Advanced Placement (AP) students, 72 percent scored a 3 or higher (which normally makes the student eligible for college credit) on at least one exam, better than state (71 percent) and national (57.8 percent) averages. About 98 percent of Archdiocese students graduate, and 96 percent of graduates go to college.

The Enrollment Slump and a Rebound

Yet business is slumping at many of the Archdiocese's high schools. Enrollment fell 11 percent from 2002 to 2017. And the Archdiocese lost more than 5,000 students the summer after the COVID-19 pandemic started.

However, enrollment figures appear to be turning around. Perhaps in part because of the pandemic's impact on learning routines in public schools throughout Boston, nearly 1,400 new students enrolled in the Archdiocese of Boston's schools for the 2021–2022 school year, according to data provided by the Archdiocese.

The biggest increase for 2021–2022 came from elementary students, where enrollment climbed from 17,108 students last year to 18,256 students this year. And enrollment at parochial schools, specifically, increased from 12,840 students a year ago to 13,652 students this year.

Many former Catholic school families are moving to the suburbs and sending their children to public high schools. Catholic school payrolls have risen as nuns and priests have been replaced by lay teachers. And the clergy abuse scandal meant the end of archdiocesan subsidies. That has left the schools — ineligible for public funding — to rely on tuitions, fundraising, and grants.

Meanwhile, voc-tech education in Massachusetts has surged, in part because a 1993 reform measure required voc-tech students to pass the same Massachusetts Comprehensive Assessment

System (MCAS) tests as college prep students. Voc-tech dropout rates are significantly lower than traditional high schools, and students often have a job waiting upon graduation. Waiting lists have swelled into the thousands.[46]

Taking Another Look at Voc-Tech

Catholic education leaders have noticed the rise in voc-tech popularity and understand the economic opportunities that await graduates, but they worry about blurring their reputation for college preparation. Nationwide, Catholic school seniors score an average of 20 and 26 points higher in math and reading than their public school counterparts on the National Assessment of Educational Progress (NAEP), and an average 45, 43, and 53 points higher on math, reading, and writing SAT assessments, respectively.[47]

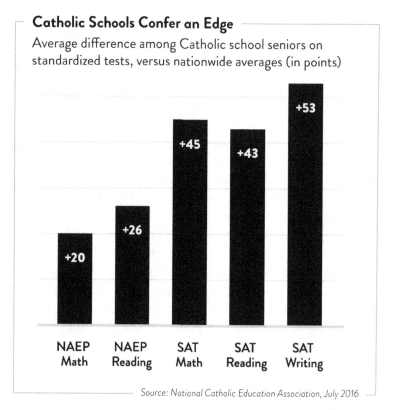

Catholic Schools Confer an Edge

Average difference among Catholic school seniors on standardized tests, versus nationwide averages (in points)

- NAEP Math: +20
- NAEP Reading: +26
- SAT Math: +45
- SAT Reading: +43
- SAT Writing: +53

Source: National Catholic Education Association, July 2016

"That has always been the brand that has identified us, so there has been a little bit of pause when you think about the public perception if we were to introduce vocational education into a Catholic high school," said Heather Gossart, senior consultant with the National Catholic Education Association.[48]

In 2017, the Archdiocese of Boston commissioned a study to explore voc-tech education. Then-superintendent Kathy Mears thought it was a good idea.

"There's a New England bias looking down on vocational education," she said. "But the Catholic Church believes in the dignity of work and that all work is good. There is no shame in not having a degree from Harvard."[49]

This chapter explores the merits of and financial and facilities requirements of medical voc-tech education for Catholic high schools. Health services include nurse aide training, dental assisting, medical laboratory assisting, and electrocardiogram (EKG) technician training.

There is only one traditional career voc-tech education Catholic high school in the U.S.—Mercy Career & Technical High School in Philadelphia. There have been others, including Don Bosco Technical High School in Boston, which closed in 1998. Voc-tech instruction in Catholic schools today means programs in computer science or biotechnology at college prep schools. Yet that may be about to change.

Background

Since seeing enrollment peak in the early 1960s—when more than 5.2 million students attended nearly 13,000 Catholic schools nationwide—Catholic school enrollments have declined, and many schools have closed.

But as Archdiocese of Boston schools have struggled, the number of students in voc-tech education has been climbing. In 2011, there were 44,175 students in Chapter 74-approved programs in regional voc-tech, district vocational, or traditional public high schools. By 2018, there were 48,750, a 10.4 percent increase over 2011. A decade later, in 2021, there were more than 50,000 students.[50]

David Ferreira, former executive director of the Massachusetts Association of Vocational Administrators (MAVA), said the increase was probably limited by lack of sufficient seats to meet demand.[51]

Politicians and business leaders view voc-tech education as a way to raise employment and address a skilled labor shortage. In January 2016, Governor Charlie Baker announced $83.5 million in funding for career vocational education over five years,[52] including $9.3 million in workforce skills equipment grants to 35 high schools, community colleges, and vocational training providers.

As of 2021, more than $30 million had been awarded.

The state also provided another $11.8 million in taxpayer revenue in March 2017 for 32 vocational schools, community colleges, and traditional public high schools to purchase equipment and expand training.[53]

A coalition of business groups, community organizations, and vocational high school administrators formed the Alliance for Vocational Technical Education to promote voc-tech education. They raised $60,000 to fund a study at Northeastern University about public perceptions of these schools.[54] A 2016 survey of more than 350 Massachusetts employers found some 90 percent saw a need to increase the number of voc-tech graduates and provide voc-tech schools with more modern equipment.[55]

Promise in the Health Services

The Commonwealth's voc-tech health services cluster includes health, dental, and medical assisting. Students typically prepare for the American Red Cross Certified Nursing Assistant Exam, the National Health Career Association National Certification Exam for EKG Technicians, and the American Heart Association First Aid Certification.

In Massachusetts, 25 of 26 regional voc-tech schools offer courses in the health assisting cluster.[56] Enrollment in health services rose nearly 17 percent from 2011 to 2017, according to the state Department of Elementary and Secondary Education (DESE).

According to the latest research from the Massachusetts Executive Office of Workforce and Labor Development, there is a growing need for health and allied health professionals throughout the Commonwealth. Teaching certificate courses in Catholic high schools is a way to ensure both immediate career entry for graduates or a solid background for postsecondary study in the medical arts and sciences.

Students who complete a four-year health assisting program are prepared for entry-level positions leading to careers as an EMT, occupational therapist, or registered nurse. From 2020 to 2030, demand in Massachusetts for home health aides is expected to rise more than 33 percent; for medical assistants, 18 percent; and for physical therapists more than 21 percent.[57]

The High Price of Voc-Tech

Tempting as those numbers are, the typical cost to educate a voc-tech student is $16,945 per year, about 54 percent above the average cost per student in a Boston Archdiocese high school. Attracting private-sector professionals also requires higher teacher salaries. Frequent upgrades are required to maintain equipment in programs such as advanced manufacturing or heating, ventilation, and air conditioning. Minimum size requirements are needed to comply with student-teacher ratios.

A health assisting program is among the least expensive voc-tech programs, but it's still not cheap:

- At Assabet Valley Regional Technical High School in Marlborough, the fiscal 2017 budget for health technologies was $340,652, according to Superintendent Ernest Houle. About $336,000 of that was for salaries.[58]
- At Bay Path Regional Vocational Technical High School in Charlton, 80 students are in the health assisting program, and salaries for four instructors totaled $338,000 in 2018, according to Superintendent John Lafleche. A new dental program required about $300,000 to outfit the lab. The instructor salary was $61,000.[59]
- Minuteman Regional Vocational Technical High School

in Lexington built a new school. Superintendent Edward A. Bouquillon estimated $10,000 per student for furniture, fixtures, and equipment—at least $150,000 for a 15-student shop program in the first year.[60]

Public voc-tech schools enjoy taxpayer support and receive financial aid through the Carl D. Perkins Career and Technical Education grant program, federal money that can be used for staffing and equipment.

Catholic schools receive no public funds and aren't eligible for Perkins grants. Without taxpayer support, Ferreira said, it would be unrealistic to expect the Archdiocese to run a similar school, since tuition alone "is not going to be anywhere sufficient enough to provide this kind of school."[61]

Each high school in the Archdiocese raises about $200,000 to $400,000 annually through tuition and fundraising. Tuitions vary widely, and most schools provide financial aid, including discounts for siblings. At Boston College High School, for example, nearly half the students receive assistance, an average of about $8,300 annually.[62]

Along with lower enrollments and declining tuition revenue, Catholic schools have experienced a transition "from a basically free workforce in the persons of religious priests, brothers, and women" to one composed "predominantly of the laity, who rightly must receive just wages and benefits," said George Henry, former superintendent of Catholic education for the Archdiocese of St. Louis.[63]

Chris Fay, principal of Christian Brothers High School in Memphis, Tennessee, said schools are struggling to pay reasonable salaries without pricing their schools above what their families can pay.[64]

Cost-Saving Strategies

Even in a relatively low-cost voc-tech discipline such as health assisting, creating lab spaces that meet state specifications is expensive.

"Your facilities need to be a minimum size," Bouquillon said. "If the student-teacher ratio is maxed out at 15, you need at least 1,900 square feet. And if you expect to go into medical laboratory technology, you're going to need a larger shop area."

One cost-saving approach for Catholic schools could be to use the facilities of existing voc-tech schools during the school day or after hours, rather than building their own.

Mears, who was the assistant superintendent of schools at the Archdiocese of Indianapolis, saw such a partnership work in Indiana.

"We sent our kids to the public schools for voc-tech, but they still took their English, math, and other core subjects at the Catholic school," she said. "The voc-tech loved it because they counted as their students, and they got the money from the state for them."

Massachusetts voc-tech superintendents are open to working with Catholic schools, but staffing, scheduling, and financing all need to be worked out.

"If a Catholic school were located near a regional vocational school, there are models that could be used," said Lafleche.

With 40 weeks in a school year, he said, it would be easy to get 300 to 400 hours in after school.

Bouquillon said he's committed to working with traditional schools, private schools, and charter public schools. The caveat is whether the district offering a voc-tech program would be allowed to count each student and be compensated by the Commonwealth.

Lexington High School students who have passed MCAS may attend the "Minuteman in the Morning" program and return to Lexington High for the remainder of the school day. They earn a diploma from Lexington High School and a certificate from Minuteman.

Creating a Voc-Tech Program

A health services program could fit well with the Boston-area economy, with its many hospitals and employment opportunities in health care, especially for low-income students.

"If kids who are economically disadvantaged can complete some kind of certificate program in the time they graduate from high school, then they will have a job that will probably pay between $30,000 and $40,000," said Mears. "It could be a total game changer for economically disadvantaged children."[65]

But the Archdiocese faces a tall task if it commits to adding a voc-tech program. Under Chapter 74 of the state laws, public schools proposing voc-tech programs must demonstrate a need for and student interest in a program, and that the program will prepare students for high-wage, high-need jobs.

Because they are private, Catholic high schools are not required to comply with Chapter 74 regulations. But any voc-tech program in health services needs to be competitive with other schools in that space.

"If School X has 1,000 students, the only way a program like this makes sense is if now you have 1,020 students, because 20 of them came specifically for this program," said Lafleche of Bay Path. "If the tuition is $10,000 per year, there's an extra $200,000 to work with. So, if you're going to put this program in the high school and not grow your population, you're adding a heck of a lot of cost with no revenue."

When students graduate from a health assisting program, they typically hold one or more of several industry-recognized credentials, such as Certified Nursing Assistant (CNA), first aid certification, a license to operate an EKG machine, an EMT license, or perhaps a phlebotomy license. By preparing students in the allied health fields, the Archdiocese would give them an advantage in college admissions into STEM fields.

For instance, for a student who wants to be a pharmacist (current average salary nearly $113,000), what better background for admittance into the Massachusetts College of Pharmacy and Health Sciences' Doctor of Pharmacy program than a Pharm Tech Certificate? A certified background in an allied health or nursing field is a tremendous asset for any serious applicant.

High schools in Massachusetts have proven that voc-tech and college prep can be combined. Many students take AP and honors courses and go to college. But major differences remain. While Catholic school teachers are not required to be licensed by the DESE, anyone teaching in a health-related voc-tech program, public or private, must be licensed in medical areas—although there is a grace period.

"During the first year when you're operating as a non-CTE you can have a teacher with just a science background teaching it," said Victoria Kelly, career academy coordinator at Haverhill High School. "We had a biotech teacher who taught it the first year. But in order to get vocationally certified for health assisting we need an RN."[66]

Voc-tech programs must meet state-mandated teacher/student ratios. And, unlike college prep students, those attending voc-tech schools generally split their time each day between the classroom and the clinical instruction that is one of the foundational components of the voc-tech experience.

Further, health disciplines require some clinical affiliation in which a nurse goes with students to do hands-on care. While freshmen and sophomores have mock training in the laboratory, Ferreira said that students "have hands-on experience with actual patients as they become juniors and seniors."

Students must record a minimum of 120 hours of lab work and pass an exam to qualify as a CNA, but it's not unusual for teenagers to take longer to be trained and ready for the test.

Mercy Career & Technical High School

Mercy Career & Technical High School in Philadelphia is the nation's only coed Catholic CVTE high school. It proves that voc-tech can work for a Catholic school, but also demonstrates that it might take unique circumstances to pay for it.

Founded in 1950 by the Sisters of Mercy as a three-year certificate technical school, Mercy converted into a full high school in the 1970s. It prepares graduates for continuing education or immediate employment. Students earn a high school diploma and study to achieve industry-recognized certifications in their chosen career and technical program.

In addition to a standard academic program, Mercy has six

career technical education programs: business, building trades, computer technology, cosmetology, culinary arts, and nurse aide training.

Freshmen take a career exploration course of one period per week, which helps them make their career and technical program decisions at the end of that year. They take the CVTE curriculum for the next three years and may participate as seniors in the school's co-op program. Mercy reports 99 percent graduation and 97 percent attendance rates.[67]

Much like Catholic high schools in Boston, tuition alone could not support the CVTE program at Mercy. Tuition is $8,640, but the cost to educate each student is more than $14,000, and more than 90 percent of Mercy's students qualify for assistance.[68]

As a private school, Mercy does not receive state taxpayer funds, federal Perkins money, or an allowance from the Archdiocese of Philadelphia. But Mercy does benefit from state tax laws and agreements.

In 2016, the school raised more than $1.86 million in gifts, including $353,500 received through Pennsylvania's Educational Improvement Tax Credit (EITC) and Opportunity Scholarship Tax Credit (OSTC) programs, which extend tax credits to businesses contributing to scholarship organizations.

In the 2015–2016 school year, 48 Mercy families received tuition assistance through the EITC and nearly 100 families through the OSTC.[69]

Since 1992, Mercy has also shared in an annual $1.5 million fund from the Pennsylvania Convention Center. In 2016, Mercy's gift of $278,667 financed core training in the building trades, business education, and culinary arts.

In October 2021, despite the COVID-19 pandemic, the school's annual fall fundraiser generated $370,000.

Mercy's Nurse Aide Training Program (NATP) prepares students for health careers over a period of three academic years. At the end of their junior year, students qualify to take the Pennsylvania Nurse Aide Certification examination.[25]

"We're looking to add more to that program," said Catherine

Glatts, vice principal of technology and career and technical education. "We could teach medical coding and medical assistance. Those aren't expensive. Our nursing is long-term care. We're looking to also bring in acute care."

Mercy partners with local businesses and others for materials and co-op opportunities. In 2016, Local 98 of the International Brotherhood of Electrical Workers donated materials that Mercy students could not afford. In return, the IBEW and other business partners use Mercy's facilities during after-school hours.

Conclusion

Leaders of Archdiocese of Boston high schools face challenging times. Despite a recent influx of students because of the COVID-19 pandemic, enrollment has declined in recent years at many of its schools, and the allure of a college-prep high school has faded as many college graduates struggle to get jobs. More families are turning to a career voc-tech education so their children can graduate with employable skills and a solid foundation for higher education.

In response, Catholic high schools are considering breaking from tradition to incorporate voc-tech education. The preferred discipline would be health care, given the enormous employment base that exists in metropolitan Boston.

But the money issue is still significant. Tuition revenue is inadequate to cover costs, fundraising income varies among the 30 high schools, and the Archdiocese of Boston does not provide any financial assistance.

The Catholic Schools Office has commissioned a study to help determine whether there is strong enough demand among families of prospective students to add voc-tech to the curriculum.

Recommendations
Repeal Massachusetts's two Anti-Aid Amendments

Repeal of Anti-Aid or Know-Nothing Amendments to the Massachusetts Constitution is essential to helping close the enormous gap between the ability of Massachusetts's regional career voc-tech schools to offer programs and that of Catholic high schools to do so. The Supreme Court of the United States' 2020 decision in *Espinoza v. Montana Department of Revenue* may not directly affect the state's Anti-Aid Amendments, but it provides encouragement for the Commonwealth to head in that direction.

Explore a partnership between the Archdiocese and regional voc-tech schools

Startup costs, even for relatively low-budget health care programs, can run into the hundreds of thousands of dollars. Regional voc-tech superintendents are open to cooperation with Catholic high schools. Catholic school voc-tech students could split their day between a voc-tech school and their Catholic high school. Using public school facilities would enable Catholic schools to begin a voc-tech program while creating their own lab space in a way that is financially feasible.

Investigate start-up assistance organizations

To mitigate startup costs, school could turn to licensed organizations that handle the heavy lifting for a school that wants to add nursing and allied health programs. Setting up new programs is a huge commitment but using proven programs can get the process going very quickly.

Meet Chapter 74 requirements

Catholic high schools are not required to meet state Chapter 74 standards for voc-tech education but would be more competitive if they did. The "Chapter 74 Manual for Vocational Technical Education Programs," published by the Massachusetts DESE, is a resource for school districts in the implementation of voc-tech programs.

■ ■ ■

Alison L. Fraser is an education policy, research, and strategy consultant and president of Practical Policy. Previously, she was an administrator at Blackstone Valley Tech and director of policy and advocacy at Mass Insight Education, where she directed the Great Schools Campaign and development of No Excuses for Failing Schools and Excellence in Math and Science Goals. An expert in standards-based curriculum, Fraser has coordinated activities and programs for the Coalition for Higher Standards and led research in standards-based reform.

William Donovan is a former staff writer with the Providence Journal in Rhode Island, where he wrote about business and government. He has taught business journalism in the graduate programs at Boston University and Northeastern University. He received his undergraduate degree from Boston College and his master's degree in Journalism from American University in Washington, D.C.

Chapter 5
Madison Park Technical Vocational High School Turnaround

by William Donovan

Madison Park Technical Vocational High School in Boston is attempting a turnaround and has been for decades. In 2016, after having been designated a Level 4 school by the Massachusetts Department of Elementary and Secondary Education (DESE), a stamp that branded it underperforming, school officials created a plan they began implementing in June of that year.

The turnaround plan was a 111-page document that included a stark look at recent poor practices — and some unique challenges — at the school, which was founded in 1977. More importantly, the document included a strategy to change the culture at Madison Park, stimulate academic improvement, provide more professional support for teachers, and reverse rising dropout and falling graduation rates.

Since the new plan began, some signs of improvement have appeared. The graduation rate, which was 57 percent in 2017, was above 68 percent in 2019. The dropout rate, once above 6 percent, is now under 5 percent. Enrollment, which tumbled by half from 2005 to 2017, has climbed more than 17 percent in the past three years.

Advanced instruction has emerged as a strong point for the school. Dual enrollment partnerships with several local colleges have enabled many Madison Park students to earn college credits before graduating.

Madison Park has struggled with frequent leadership turnover. Between 2010 and 2015, the school had five different headmasters.

In 2020, two students earned their associate degree. Early results of the turnaround project have been recognized by the New England Association of Schools and Colleges (NEASC). In late 2018, NEASC reported in the evaluation it conducts of schools every 10 years that Madison Park was "poised to establish itself as an institution of first-class learning."

If that evaluation comes to pass, it will represent a significant comeback. Despite the encouraging indicators, the school still trails other voc-tech schools in the state in academics. Its Massachusetts Comprehensive Assessment System (MCAS) scores rank at or near the bottom in all categories. It is the worst performer among them in terms of graduation and dropout rates, trailing the statewide average in those categories among voc-tech schools by large margins.

The attempted turnaround is also happening at a time when the Boston Public Schools (BPS) are under fire. In March 2020, the DESE released a highly critical review of the Boston system. It concluded that students in the district faced transportation problems, poor facilities, excessive leadership turnover, considerable disparities in access to resources, and "systemic disarray" of special education services.[70]

Madison Park has struggled with frequent leadership turnover. Between 2010 and 2015, the school had five different headmasters. Another headmaster was removed in May 2020 as part of a citywide shake-up among school administrations.

At the same time, it was announced that Kevin McCaskill, who has led the turnaround effort over the last five years as the school's executive director, would be moving to the BPS central office to assume broader responsibilities.

McCaskill remained executive director and interim headmaster until Dr. Sidney Brown was appointed as headmaster in the summer of 2021.

Each new principal brought new priorities and approaches, interrupting continuity in planning and effort. In particular, after a much-heralded innovation plan was approved in 2012, BPS invested more than $1 million in technology, textbooks, and voc-tech materials.[71] But as leadership changed, support for the plan waned.

The challenges for Madison Park go beyond the headmaster's office.

Absenteeism remains high, with 47 percent of students missing 10 percent or more of school days in 2018–2019.

During the 2019–2020 school year, 92 percent of the 1,021 students enrolled at Madison Park were classified as "high needs." That was second only to Boston International High School, a college preparatory school designed to teach students English, including a program for students newly arrived in the U.S. who have little or no schooling in their home country or whose education has been interrupted.

In the 2018–2019 school year, 73.1 percent of Madison Park's students were considered economically disadvantaged, the highest among voc-tech schools in the state. Roughly 35 percent were English Language Learners, again the highest among voc-tech schools, and 30.6 percent had disabilities, according to DESE.

Absenteeism remains high, with 47 percent of students missing 10 percent or more of school days in 2018–2019. Those numbers certainly contribute to underperformance at urban college preparatory high schools. But they are more of a factor at urban voc-tech schools. There, students who are English Language Learners must often negotiate textbooks that are more exacting and precise than college textbooks, creating a greater need for remedial services.

Demographics can create a difficult apples-to-oranges comparison when Madison Park is compared with schools whose enrollment includes fewer students learning English, fewer students from disadvantaged communities, and more students from higher-income backgrounds.

Many of the top performing voc-tech schools in Massachusetts are in upper-income suburban communities or rural areas. Still, other urban voc-tech schools, such as Lynn Vocational Technical Institute and the Roger L. Putnam Vocational Technical Academy in Springfield—where McCaskill previously led reforms—have large low-income, English Language Learner populations, and have managed to raise academic scores and graduation rates, while also seeing a decline in dropouts.

The question, then, is this: Can Madison Park play a larger role in creating educational and economic opportunity in Boston by providing needed skilled labor for Boston-based businesses?

As noted, McCaskill was the principal at Putnam when it began its turnaround. But he said he's aiming higher than Putnam or Lynn Tech and wants to outperform top Massachusetts voc-tech schools such as Valley Tech in Upton and Assabet Valley in Marlborough, both of which serve communities that are very distinct from Boston.

"I compare our data against what I consider the best vocational system in the country," said McCaskill. "We're behind with respect to performance of students. But that's the only way you catch up. Compare yourself to the best. Even though their demographics are nowhere near ours, nowhere near it, those are the schools we want to be compared to."[72]

Background

In the past 20 years, there has been a resurgence of interest in career voc-tech education. States have more than 100 new laws, policies, and regulations related to vocational education, many of which increased state funding for such programs.[73]

A 2015 University of Connecticut study found that full-time voc-tech schools in Massachusetts—as opposed to college preparatory high schools that embed some voc-tech courses in their curriculum—successfully promote improved graduation rates and lower dropout rates.[74]

Other reports have found that students who received voc-tech training scored higher on math exams. Also, attendance and graduation rates at voc-tech schools were generally above 90 percent, and there were particularly strong benefits for low-income students.[75]

Together, these results speak to the reputation that voc-tech schools are developing as places where students can graduate equipped with practical skills and preparation for higher education.

Madison Park, located in the Roxbury neighborhood of Boston, is a grade 9–12 high school, with more than 1,000 students in the 2019–2020 school year. It is the only school in Boston that exclusively prepares its students for careers and postsecondary education upon graduation.

Madison Park offers training in 20 programs, including Automotive Technology, Dental Assisting, Graphic Communications, Culinary Arts, Carpentry, and Programming and Web Development.

During their freshman year, students explore all programs and select a concentration. All students rotate their schedule every other week.

Freshmen and sophomores alternate one full week of academic courses with a week in which they spend half of each day in voc-tech education. Juniors and seniors rotate a full week of academic courses with a week of full-time voc-tech education.

Madison Park is a citywide option for high school students. Every Boston neighborhood is represented at the school, but more than 80 percent of the enrollment comes from five neighborhoods: Dorchester, Roxbury, East Boston, Mattapan, and Hyde Park.

The school does not have an admissions policy. Students are placed there through the BPS school selection process.

In his 2012 State of the City address, the late Boston Mayor Thomas M. Menino called Madison Park "one of our most important city assets," which "should be the pathway to solid jobs and a strong future for city youth."[76]

Trailing in Academics and Co-op Programs

But as he spoke, Madison Park was far from being a successful voc-tech school. For every 11 students at Madison Park at the time, just one was involved in a work-based cooperative. The average student was absent for more than one month out of every year.[77]

Academically, only 9 percent of students scored in the Advanced category on MCAS math exams, while 27.6 percent scored Proficient, 36 percent scored Needs Improvement, and more than 26 percent finished in the Warning/Failing category.

On the English exam, only 1.6 percent scored Advanced, nearly 47 percent were Proficient, nearly 42 percent were in the Needs Improvement category, and 10 percent in Warning/ Failing.

In the years that followed, the numbers did not radically change. Around the same time Madison Park entered a period of leadership instability.

- A long-serving headmaster retired with little notice at the end of the 2011–2012 school year, leaving the school to begin the next year with an interim headmaster.
- The interim headmaster was eventually removed amid a federal probe of his alleged role in a multistate credit fraud ring. (No criminal charges were filed.)
- Another headmaster, who had been on the job for a year, resigned after the school department discovered she never gained certification to lead a school in Massachusetts.[78]
- The next headmaster was placed on leave slightly more than two years later for undisclosed reasons.

- The fifth headmaster was removed in May 2020 when changes were made at several Boston high schools.

A Study Board and Recommendations Emerge

In March 2014, the interim superintendent of the Boston Public Schools and the Boston Teachers Union announced an intervention at Madison Park. A seven-person board was created to study the school.

Four months later, it produced a report that included 27 recommendations, including shutting the school down in three years and replacing it with an independent regional vocational school unless improvements were made.[79]

In August 2014, the school was scrambling to hire dozens of new teachers and administrators before classes started, then opened in September with no schedules ready for students or teachers.[80]

In December 2015, the state made its Level 4 determination following an analysis of four-year trends in absolute achievement, student growth, and academic improvement. School officials were then required to develop a turnaround plan, which was completed in June 2016.

The turmoil at Madison Park has often prompted critics to dismiss the school. But others suggest that BPS isn't fully committed to its success.

The 2018 NEASC report noted:

"The wide dispersal of technical programs throughout the city, including the duplication of programs already in existence, has decreased demand for programs at [Madison Park]. In turn, this has helped depress enrollment. ... The team further finds that efforts to create dozens of additional technical programs elsewhere in the city, while perhaps started with the best of intentions, has served to help create uncertainty about [Madison Park], its importance to the city and its future as an educational institution."[81]

The Turnaround Plan

Madison Park is implementing a turnaround plan within a broader partnership that was established in March 2020 between DESE and the BPS.

In the agreement, BPS agreed to deliver measurable results on four priority initiatives drawn from the findings of the district review. DESE agreed to support BPS on four complementary initiatives.

During the next three years, "a major focus of the district will be on making measurable improvements in the 33 schools that face the most challenges in student achievement ... Boston Public Schools will also address student success in high school, programming for students with disabilities, English Language Learners and transportation challenges."[82]

This effort is certain to involve Madison Park, with its large high-needs student population. In broad terms, the 2016 turnaround plan was aimed at the culture at Madison Park. Priorities included the uncertainty in leadership, addressing the special needs of the student body, and providing teachers with the professional development opportunities and time they lacked.

"The goal over the next three years is to stabilize the school through the commitment of a skilled and dedicated staff who will create a dynamic learning environment that prepares students for postsecondary success in academia and career pathways," the plan stated.[83]

The turnaround plan was written by representatives from Madison Park, including McCaskill and others within the BPS administration. The plan made the case for consistent leadership by pointing out the negative impact on staff of the frequent changes in the headmaster's office.

The Impact of Frequent Leadership Changes

According to the 2016 monitoring site visit annual report for Madison Park—conducted by the American Institutes for Research—there was a lack of "guiding vision" at the school.[84]

"I think the hard thing about having a new headmaster every

year or half a year in some instances," one teacher said, "is that it makes it so that teachers don't want to spend their time planning things or doing things because … it's made no difference for the next year. You work for a whole year doing something and then the next year you have someone new who doesn't know anything about that and so your work just goes out the window."[85]

That view was also apparent in Madison Park's results on the Fall 2015 TNTP Instructional Culture INSIGHT survey, which provides leaders feedback on aspects of school culture that are important for teacher and student success.

Only 29 percent of respondents affirmed that "When my school leadership commits to a program or priority, they follow through."[86]

Peter Dewar, retired assistant executive director of the Massachusetts Association of Vocational Administrators (MAVA), credits McCaskill for addressing the turnover problem by sending Madison Park personnel to Leadership Academies at MAVA.

The courses are "highly successful in creating folks ready for the next job when it materializes," said Dewar. "That's been the key to success across the state."

McCaskill said nine teachers have completed or are currently enrolled in the MAVA Leadership Academies. One assumed a vocational director position at another BPS school, and another was elevated from vocational instructor to co-op coordinator.

What's Changing?

So, what is the plan and what has happened since 2016? McCaskill said the program has not been 100 percent implemented. Budgetary issues prevented him from filling certain positions early on. The 2018 NEASC report noted that per-pupil expenditures for Madison Park were $18,242 in FY2019, lower than all but one of eight comparable voc-tech high schools in the region, and well below the average per-pupil spending of $23,247 at those schools.

Proper funding is also important for Madison Park because of the demand for extra services that results when 92 percent of the students enrolled are considered to have high needs. The examiners in the NEASC study wrote: "…with the high number of students requiring support services, at risk, or special ed/504 services, staffing is less than adequate. Seventy-two percent of Madison Park students are identified at intervention level based."

Two-thirds of all students are identified as special education or in need of ELL services. The school psychologist conducted a significant number of suicide assessments in the 2017–2018 school year. The report noted that although Madison Park has more than 300 students in need of English Language Learning, there is a shortage of bilingual teachers, specifically in the trade areas, where a paraprofessional is utilized to support instruction, among other responsibilities.[87]

Underinvestment at Madison Park

Per-pupil expenditures FY2019: $18,242

21.4% below average for comparable schools in region

Source: 2018 NEASC report

In the turnaround plan, school officials wrote that improving student performance and achievement was at "the foundation" of their design.[88] Unquestionably, academics need to improve before Madison Park can become the local economic powerhouse its backers want it to be.

Under the plan, the elements of that foundation include:

- **Creating small learning communities (SLCs).** SLCs are meant to build a strong and supportive culture among teachers and students and promote the integration of academics and voc-tech education.

- **Establishing a supportive network for students and their families.** These networks are within the small learning communities. Not only do they lift student achievement, but they also foster open lines of communication to families and elevate students' overall well-being.

- **Enhancing community partnerships.** Stronger community partnerships are expected to lead to increased opportunities for shadowing, internships, and employment, as well as providing student support wraparound services. Wraparound services in schools are designed to give a student academic, social, and behavioral assistance throughout the school day.

A comprehensive approach of this sort—small, focused groups with clear communication between academics and vocational instruction, and inclusive of families—is vital when the percentage of high-needs students at Madison Park is equal to what alternative schools have, according to McCaskill.

Small, concentrated groups can also help address other problems, such as Madison Park's chronically high absenteeism. In the turnaround plan, student attendance was highlighted as a priority. The average Madison Park student missed 21.5 days of school and 45 percent of all students qualified as chronically absent during the 2014–2015 school year.[89]

In the 2018–2019 school year, the chronic absenteeism rate, meaning the percentage of students who have missed 10 percent or more of school days, was 47 percent. In the 2019–2020 year, the number was down to 32 percent, according to McCaskill.

MCAS Bootcamp to Support Students

One example of academic support available to students, according to the NEASC study, is MCAS Bootcamp, an opportunity for students to strengthen their skills in math, English Language Arts (ELA), or science for the MCAS exams.

The program involves learning test-taking strategies, practicing open response writing, and studying the academic language they need to understand the test questions.

MCAS Bootcamp is open to all students, including those on an Individualized Education Program (IEP). MCAS Bootcamp began when McCaskill became executive director in 2015. Since then, math and ELA scores have been mixed.

Students have produced their most consistent success rates in science. There, the percentage of students scoring Advanced has ticked up slightly, to 2.7 percent in the 2019 exam. But the percentage of those scoring Proficient rose to 25.7 percent from 11.9 percent in 2018 and those in the Needs Improvement fell to 48 percent from 60.1 percent.

The Warning/Failing improvement was less dramatic, but still a gain, falling from 28 percent in 2018 to 23.6 percent in 2019.

"From a teaching and learning perspective, a lot of work has gone in, and we just haven't seen the traction yet," said McCaskill. "We have seen it in science. Math has been up and down, as well as English Language Arts."

But when analyzing Madison Park's MCAS scores, McCaskill says people too often are not considering the school's population. Some students enter their freshman year reading at a fifth and sixth grade level.

"When we have moved the needle, it's to the point where people say, 'Yeah, but you're still below the average,' " he said. "They're not looking at the improvement... But that's when you do have to look at the actual demographics."

Another academic support initiative has been the pre-Advanced Placement (AP) courses started in 2016 for freshmen and sophomores to prepare them for AP courses. A team of 9th grade teachers received pre-AP training from Mass Insight Education and Research, an organization that has worked to help Boston Public School students succeed in pre-AP and AP courses.

Members on that team then led a workshop for their colleagues at the start of the school year. AP courses at Madison Park include English Language Arts, Biology and Physics.

The NEASC report stated that most Madison Park students feel supported by the administration and staff when faced with difficult academic challenges.

"I'm from Colombia," one 11th grade student said. "This school gave me the support I needed to build my English. They provided me with an interpreter in my freshman year and MCAS Bootcamp. It made me feel confident, like I could do it... and I did."[90]

Credits for College

One program that has demonstrated success has been the Roxbury Massachusetts Advanced Post-Secondary Pathways (RoxMAPP), in which students take college-level courses and earn college credit while attending Madison Park.

RoxMAPP is a dual enrollment/early college program for students in grades 10–12. Students can earn up to 15 transferable college credits at local colleges, including Bunker Hill Community College, Roxbury Community College, Wentworth Institute of Technology, and Benjamin Franklin Institute of Technology (BFIT).

Since the 2014–2015 school year, the number of students participating in RoxMAPP has risen from 15 to 83, and the total number of college credits earned has jumped from 45 to 716.[91]

In 2020, two students earned an associate degree before they graduated from Madison Park. One student's degree was in liberal arts from Bunker Hill Community College; the other's was in biomedical engineering technology from BFIT.

In addition to letting students earn credits and degrees, RoxMAPP gives students a head start on their college and career exploration. They experience life on a college campus, and the credits they've earned are worth thousands of dollars at the rates they would pay if taking the same courses after leaving Madison Park.

The Lynn Tech Turnaround: It Starts at the Top

No two schools are perfectly alike, but they can be similar. In 2019, there were 1,026 students at Lynn Vocational Technical Institute in Lynn. Seventy-two percent of the students were considered high needs and English was a second language for more than 63 percent of them.

Ten years ago, the dropout rate at Lynn Tech was 7 percent and the graduation rate was 59 percent. Since then, those numbers have changed substantially. The dropout rate in 2019 was down to 0.6 percent and the graduation rate was up to 89.5 percent.

What happened?

In 2009, Dr. Catherine Latham, a new Lynn superintendent of schools, threw her support behind improving Lynn Tech. The school had done poorly in an inspection by the state DESE's Co-ordinated Program Review (CPR).

Through the CPR, the state oversees local compliance with education requirements in several areas, including special education, civil rights, and career voc-tech education. The state required corrective action by Lynn Tech following the review.

A second evaluation, the 10-year assessment by NEASC, also recommended changes. At the suggestion of MAVA, Latham brought in Kathleen Conole, former director of curriculum and instruction at Greater Lowell Technical High School, as a consultant. Conole worked with Lynn Tech for 18 months to implement the corrective actions.

Latham also authorized creation of a new position of MCAS coordinator, who oversaw teacher training and gathered and analyzed data on MCAS results. In addition, Latham brought in a new co-op director, who struck up new articulation agreements with colleges for students to earn credits.

Conole said the improvement was only possible because of support from the superintendent.

"If you want change in a school, it has to come from the top," she said. "There needs to be a superintendent committed to getting their hands dirty. You need someone who recognizes what needs to be done and empowers people to do it."

Latham retired in 2018. Her successor was Lynn's Deputy Superintendent, Dr. Patrick Tutwiler, assuring continuity of support for Lynn Tech. Carissa Karakaedos, a former teacher at Lynn Tech, took over as principal in 2018. Her predecessor had been principal for three years, but at the school for more than 30.

"The district has been amazing," said Karakaedos, who has had the administration's backing for a five-year plan she proposed upon becoming principal. "The superintendent and my deputy have been so supportive."

Lynn Tech had 659 applications for 340 spots in its freshman class in 2020, which Karakaedos attributes, in large part, to the five-year roadmap. Karakaedos was succeeded by Fred Gallo for the 2021–2022 school year.

Summary

COVID-19 has made educating students a challenge for even the most exceptional schools. But it's more problematic for a school such as Madison Park as it works on becoming, as Mayor Menino once said, one of Boston's "most important city assets."

Madison Park's enrollment has bounced back in recent years, after a long, steep decline. More students are graduating and fewer dropping out. There's hope that a comprehensive turnaround plan begun in 2016 will eventually produce more skilled workers to fill job openings with Boston businesses.

Although the state DESE has designated Madison Park a Level 4, or underperforming school, a team of examiners from NEASC concluded in the fall of 2018 that Madison Park "has the capacity as a learning organization to progress toward a Level 2 or Level 1 school."[92]

Despite the encouraging signs, much work needs to be done to reach those classifications. MCAS scores in science have improved, but math and ELA remain disappointing. Just when there seemed to be stability in the main office, school headmaster Brett Dickens was removed in May 2020 as part of a shuffling among leaders at several Boston high schools. Kevin McCaskill was given additional responsibilities in the Boston Public Schools central office.

In 2021, Dr. Sidney Brown was named the new headmaster at Madison Park.

It remains to be seen how the coronavirus will affect Madison Park's turnaround effort, especially given the school's high-needs student population. All schools will be assessing how the pandemic has negatively impacted their students. Madison Park will also be determining how the pandemic complicates intended outcomes based on the steps included in its turnaround plan.

McCaskill said educators will need to examine how changes in instruction during the pandemic will affect high-maintenance students who require more support.

"Some students might not have the right medium of learning available to them," McCaskill said. "It's not a matter of not having the technology. Is that the right medium for them when more hands-on, more tactile, or more face-to-face learning is their most effective mode to be educated? That's been taken away."

Recommendations

Allow more autonomy at Madison Park

There are 26 regional voc-tech schools in the MAVA network. Like them, Madison Park needs to be an independent district with its own superintendent and school committee. Allowing more autonomy would enable Madison Park to sharpen its profile as a standout voc-tech high school.

Opponents note that Boston would still need to fund Madison Park's $15 million to $20 million budget. They argue that if Madison Park were an independent, regional school, it might attract students from other communities who would take seats intended for inner-city students.

Finally, there is a blatant bias that holds Madison Park hasn't earned the opportunity to be an independent school considering its history of underperforming academically. But more autonomy in some form could open the door to more entrepreneurial management and academic growth at Madison Park.

The superintendent of BPS needs to be a Madison Park champion

The turnaround at Lynn Tech was driven by support from Lynn's superintendent of schools. If Madison Park is to produce needed skilled labor for Boston-based businesses, the impetus must come from the top.

The city's superintendent needs to become a champion and be held accountable for improving the city's only dedicated voc-tech school. But the spring shuffling of principals among several Boston high schools once again left Madison Park without a permanent headmaster just as the school prepared for opening amid a pandemic.

And the departure of BPS Superintendent Brenda Cassellius — who announced early in 2022 that she will depart in June 2022 after three years on the job — leaves a vacancy and further questions as to whether Madison Park will receive the attention and autonomy it needs in order to succeed.

How Dr. Brown handles Madison Park's challenges—including the need to build a strong relationship with incoming BPS leadership—will be critical for Madison Park in the years ahead.

Expand staff for greater support to students with special needs

During the 2015–2016 school year, the most recent prior to release of the 2016 turnaround plan, the Madison Park staff was "unprepared to address students with special needs."[93] According to the turnaround plan:

- In addition to a lack of knowledge and skills around creating new supports, staff also may not fully understand the supports Madison Park already offers.
- Madison Park has not provided consistent services to allow students with disabilities and ELLs to fully participate in our academic and CTE programs.
- Madison Park's staff lacks training in how to support all students in accessing the school's programs fully.
- Madison Park lacks protocols to guide implementation and monitoring of our student supports.

Serious attention to at-risk students can make a difference when addressing issues such as attendance, discipline, and graduation rates. With added staff, student services, rather than being reactive, can become more proactive and responsive to students' needs.

Madison Park is underfunded compared to other voc-tech schools in Massachusetts. The school should be provided resources to increase the number of certified/licensed personnel required to fully serve its student population.

Approve an admissions policy

Madison Park is an open enrollment school. Students are assigned through the BPS selection process, in which they list the high schools they would like to attend in order of preference. But that process has too often resulted in students being assigned to Madison Park because it's where there was an open slot.

Consequently, many students are enrolled who have little to no interest in voc-tech education.[94] That situation can lead to lack of effort by unhappy students and an increase in absenteeism.

About 80 percent of current students selected Madison Park either first or second, due to the school's marketing and outreach to the city's middle schools and K–8 community. An admissions policy similar to those at other voc-tech schools in the state has been approved by DESE but needs local approval.

It was submitted to the Boston School Committee in 2015 but was tabled and has not been brought forward since. It needs to be revisited to ensure that students who are attending Madison Park are the ones who want to take advantage of the opportunities offered by a career voc-tech school in Massachusetts.

Review special needs placements

Part of establishing an admissions policy requires BPS to evaluate how special education placements are made at Madison Park. It should be a place where special needs placements are appropriate, and special needs students can access high-quality programs.

Ensure BPS voc-tech programs are aligned, not duplicative

The 2018 NEASC report noted voc-tech programs have been encouraged for at least 22 other Boston high schools, some of which mirror programs already offered at Madison Park. The BPS needs to ensure that voc-tech programs across BPS schools are aligned, and not duplicative.

Expand early college options

RoxMAPP has become a success at Madison Park with Bunker Hill Community College, Roxbury Community College, Wentworth Institute of Technology, and Benjamin Franklin Institute of Technology. Not only are students getting an early start on their college degrees, but they are also saving money by earning credits while at Madison Park that would cost them thousands of dollars later. The program is a winner. The concept should be expanded to other local colleges.

■ ■ ■

William Donovan is a former staff writer with the Providence Journal in Rhode Island, where he wrote about business and government. He has taught business journalism in the graduate programs at Boston University and Northeastern University. He received his undergraduate degree from Boston College and his master's degree in Journalism from American University in Washington, D.C.

Chapter 6

A Tale of Two City Schools: Worcester Tech and Putnam Academy Become Models for Recovery

by William Donovan

There was a time decades ago when voc-tech high schools were wrongly considered by many people to be dumping grounds for kids who lacked the ability or ambition to attend a college-preparatory school. For the students attending them, the future was in their hands, not their heads.

That misperception has dramatically changed. Massachusetts's voc-tech schools today are as much about academics as they are about vocational skills. In fact, the two are intricately connected.

The Massachusetts voc-tech system has earned applause across the country for its unique model in which students alternate weeks in the classroom with weeks in a shop lab.

Far from reflecting low expectations and any lack of ambition, that format challenges voc-tech students to achieve more. They're still required to pass the Massachusetts Comprehensive Assessment System (MCAS) exam, just like students at college-prep high schools. Yet, because they split their schedule between trade shops and academics, they have only half the amount of time to prepare for those exams as do college-preparatory students.

Two Urban Voc-Tech Schools Showing the Way

Over the past 15 years, the reputation of the Massachusetts system has been enhanced by a remarkable turnaround by two of its members: Worcester Technical High School and the Roger L. Putnam Vocational Technical Academy in Springfield. These two urban high schools, once known for the low percentage of students who graduated and their high dropout rates, are examples of what can happen with new leadership, community investment, and committed teachers.

There were similarities between the two before their revivals. Both had and still have high numbers of low-income and special needs students. Both were housed in aging buildings, with insufficient shop labs and a degree of neglect that sent a message to teachers and students that the community didn't care. Each displayed a lack of urgency to improve academics and had students who did not perform well on the MCAS exams.

Their turnarounds have also been similar. Each was led by a new administration. Each moved into new modern facilities. Each had a change in the school culture and placed new emphasis on academics, adding Advanced Placement (AP) courses and undertaking other efforts that helped improve MCAS scores.

Their outcomes have been equally impressive. Graduation rates have soared, dropout rates have plummeted, and both schools now have long waiting lists. The histories of Worcester Tech and Putnam Academy can be instructive for other schools in need of radical change.

Worcester Technical High School
Background

Worcester Technical High School had 1,476 students enrolled for the 2021–2022 school year. About 57 percent of students are Hispanic or African American, 31 percent white, and nearly eight percent Asian.[95] The school features 23 vocational-technical programs, ranging from robotics to animal science to carpentry to culinary arts. Unlike large regional voc-tech schools that are independent of a single city or town, Worcester Tech is under the umbrella of the City of Worcester.

The school opened in 1908 as the Worcester Boys' Trade School, backed by the support of local industrialists who believed Worcester's growing economy needed more skilled workers. More than a decade later, the school merged with the all-girls David Hale Fanning Trade School and was renamed Worcester Vocational High School, a name it kept until 2006.

Two significant changes occurred that year. The first was the opening of a new $90 million building in the Belmont Hill section of Worcester. Instead of attending classes in the severely aged original structure, students moved into a state-of-the-art facility. The vocational shops were equipped with machines that enabled them to graduate with skills for immediate employment.

The second change was the appointment of Sheila Harrity as the school's principal. Harrity had been the principal at Wachusett Regional High School in nearby Holden. She arrived with a passion for voc-tech education and determination to increase the academic rigors that she was sure would help support students in their vocational areas.

The sparkling new school was the talk of Worcester. But there was skepticism about Harrity's appointment and whether she was up to the task. She had no experience running a voc-tech school.

"The vocational instructors were cautious, and they weren't sure about me," said Harrity. "I was greeted with articles in the paper saying, 'She's not a true vocational person' and didn't think I was capable of doing the job."[96]

The job was challenging because the students were generally underperforming. In 2000, 97 percent of Worcester Tech students scored in the Needs Improvement or Warning/Failing categories of the MCAS exams. Eighty-five percent of those students were in the Warning/Failing category. The English Language Arts (ELA) exam was barely better — 97 percent of the students tested in the Needs Improvement or Warning/Failing categories, with 76 percent in the Warning/Failing group.[97]

Not much had changed in the scores by the time Harrity arrived in 2006. Of the 252 students who took the ELA that year, no one scored in the Advanced or Proficient category. About 86 percent finished in the Needs Improvement or Warning/Failing categories. In the mathematics exam, about 66 percent scored in the Needs Improvement or Warning/Failing categories. Slightly more than 10 percent achieved Advanced or Proficient.

Fortunately, the prospects for the school had started to improve before 2006. In 1998, Worcester Vocational High School merged with the Worcester Public Schools. Initially, the purpose of the merger was to make the cost for a new vocational school building project eligible for a 90 percent reimbursement from the state.[98] But the merger also put more focus on academics and prompted an increase in resources for textbooks and professional development.

There was also a consensus building in the city during the 1990s that the vocational school needed a new building. In 1997, the New England Association of Schools and Colleges (NEASC) agreed. It determined that the school's original building, then nearly 90 years old, had deteriorated to such a condition that NEASC put the school's accreditation on warning status, notifying the city that accreditation could be revoked unless the facilities were brought up to date. Despite a controversial proposal and an arduous process selecting a location,[99] ground was broken in 2002, and the doors of the new school were opened in 2006.

A New Era Begins

Numerous changes were happening with the school that year. The new building was in a different part of town — Belmont Hill. The name changed from Worcester Vocational High School to Worcester Technical High School. Even the school's mascot was changed, with a bulldog replaced by an eagle.

Inside the school, Worcester Tech was reorganized into four learning academies that offered 25 career paths. Each was housed in its own building, with its own classrooms, conference centers, service areas, and industrial workspace.

Each academy replicated real-world conditions, both on the manufacturing and customer service levels.[100] They included

Alden Design and Engineering, Information Technology & Business Services, Allied Health & Human Services, and Coghlin Construction Technology.

The community had high expectations there would be a transformation at the school. Business and industry had raised $3 million to help finance the new building and had donated new equipment and materials. City officials and political leaders had negotiated for state and local funds. Parents and education officials assumed the quality of education at the school would improve. Pressure was on the new administration and the teachers to deliver.

Harrity looked at the new school with its cutting-edge technology and the fresh enthusiasm and saw "an educator's dream." She wanted to show that she had a passion for vocational education. Her mission was to increase academic rigor to support students in their vocational areas.

That was a change of attitude for Worcester Tech, where it was previously assumed graduates would simply find a job in the trades. Academics took a backseat to vocational training. The new vision for the school was that all students would graduate ready for college *and* a career. Academics and technical studies became more aligned to support student learning.

"They needed to be competent in their math and sciences to be a strong vocational person excelling in their field," Harrity said.[101]

A three-year plan was created. There were weekly administrative and instructional leadership team meetings. Each month, progress reports were given on steps to achieve the teams' goals and benchmarks.

"(Harrity) focused on data and test scores, academics. She focused on excellence and standards. She brought a positive feeling, encouragement, everyone can achieve," said Frances Meringolo, the head of the Social Studies Department, in a 2014 interview about Harrity's impact on the school.[102]

Advanced Placement courses were added to make academics more rigorous. AP Biology was the first course offered because none of the graduates from the Allied Health & Human Services Academy were getting admitted into premed undergraduate degree programs. Their course work was not considered strong enough. Seven AP courses were eventually offered, including in languages and environmental science.

Worcester Tech also began partnering with local community colleges to improve students' prospects for higher education. Instructors from Quinsigamond Community College taught Spanish I and II at Worcester Tech, helping students earn six college credits and satisfying a requirement of many four-year colleges.

Importance of Outside Financing

Fundraising and outside contributions from businesses were critical to Worcester Tech's turnaround. Of the $90 million price tag for the school, the city was able to secure $60 million in state financing. The other $30 million was raised by the Worcester Vocational Schools Advisory Board, made up of business leaders in the Worcester area. The board devised a program to attract contributions from local and national firms.

The effort was led by Edwin "Ted" Coghlin, owner of Coghlin Electrical Contractors, whom Harrity calls "the godfather of Worcester Tech." In an interview with *Worcester Business Journal* in 2006, Coghlin explained the approach.

"We started a program called Entrustments in which we would partner with a business, a manufacturer or a major supplier and that supplier would provide his equipment, his expertise, his knowledge, into the school," Coghlin said. "In return, we would give that particular supplier exclusivity as far as use of the products and the rest of it."[103]

Local companies jumped at the proposal, but so did high-tech giants such as Dell, which provided computers, and Cisco Systems, which provided network support. Each corporation's investments allowed them to advise on the equipment's instructions and have access to a facility where they could train their employees, sales staff, and prospective clients.

Another innovation was the Skyline Technical Fund, a 501(c)(3) account, created for the purpose of acquiring state-of-the-art computers and peripheral equipment. The goal was to ensure that the equipment at the school would never fall behind industry standards.

"In most school districts, when you're working on a transformational model, there are additional dollars that come with it," said Harrity. "We did not receive any. There was not an additional pot of money to create additional initiatives. We only received $200,000 per year in supplies, equipment, and for professional development from the city. So, we made use of the resources we had and the Skyline Technical Fund."

Annual Progress in Academics

Beginning in 2006, Worcester Tech showed improvement in MCAS scores and other measures. The percentage of students scoring Advanced in English Language Arts (ELA) rose from zero in 2006 to 21 percent in 2009 and has not dropped below double figures since, reaching 54.4 percent in 2018. The percentage scoring Advanced in Math rose from 10.4 percent in 2006 to 33 percent in 2009 and has remained above that level, reaching 53.4 percent in 2018.

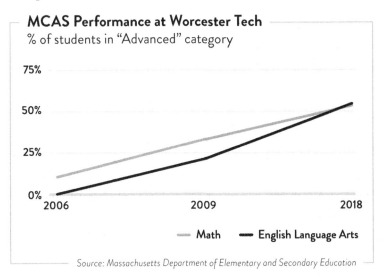

MCAS Performance at Worcester Tech
% of students in "Advanced" category

Math — English Language Arts

Source: Massachusetts Department of Elementary and Secondary Education

The graduation rate at Worcester Tech climbed dramatically, moving from 79.3 percent in 2006 to 99.1 percent in 2017. From 2018 through 2020, the average was 97.5 percent. The graduation rate for all voc-tech schools in Massachusetts during those three years was 95.5 percent.

Meanwhile, the dropout rate has fallen. In 2007, it was 8.5 percent at Worcester Tech, but only 1.1 percent by 2011. Since then, it has never risen above 1.5 percent and has averaged 1 percent annually. The dropout rate for all voc-tech schools in Massachusetts averaged 2.4 percent during that same period.

Blue Ribbon Award and President Obama's Visit

In the years following 2006, Worcester Tech received numerous national awards, including a National Breakthrough School Award in 2013 from the National Association of Secondary School Principals.

The award is given to five middle schools and five high schools each year "that serve large numbers of students living in poverty and are high achieving or dramatically improving student achievement."[104] One year later, the same organization named Harrity its National High School Principal of the Year.[105]

Worcester Tech also was given a Blue Ribbon Award from the National Blue Ribbon Schools Program, a coveted honor given by the U.S. Department of Education, which "affirms the hard work of students, educators, families, and communities in creating safe and welcoming schools where students master challenging and engaging content."[106]

The school was cited for its academic improvement and for making a difference in the community: "Student projects include construction of LEED certified low-income housing, land maintenance and water testing of public parks, and the design/fabrication of over 250 holiday wreaths that adorn downtown during the holidays — bringing great pride to students and citizens alike."[107]

The crescendo of the comeback came in 2014, when President Barack Obama gave the commencement address to the graduating class. After citing the positive changes in the school, Obama said "The thing I really want to do is make sure that what we've learned here, at this high school, we can lift up for the entire nation. I want the nation to learn from Worcester Tech."

Roger L. Putnam Vocational Technical Academy
Background

Putnam Academy is a public high school within the Springfield school system. Enrollment during the 2021–2022 school year was 1,396, with 65 percent of the students Hispanic, 20 percent African American and 10 percent white.[108] Twenty-two shop programs are offered, including Automotive Technology, Cosmetology, Information Support Services, and Robotics and Automation.[109]

Enrollment at Putnam Vocational Technical Academy in Springfield

+66.2% between 2003 and 2008

Source: *Massachusetts Department of Elementary and Secondary Education*

The school opened in 1938 as Springfield Trade School. The name was changed to Springfield Trade High School, and later to Roger L. Putnam Vocational Technical High School in honor of a former city mayor. In 2012, it became known as Roger L. Putnam Vocational Technical Academy.

In 2006, the dropout rate was 33.5 percent, higher than all voc-tech schools in Massachusetts and far above the average 11.2 percent rate for the group. The graduation rate that year was 49.2 percent, second lowest in the state and far behind the 80.7 percent average for the state's voc-tech schools. In fact, Putnam Academy's graduate rate was higher than only one other school, Madison Park Technical Vocational High School in Boston.

But 2006 represented the low point in Putnam Academy's

recent history. Improvement came slowly at first, then with a rush. Like Worcester Tech, the changes were ushered in by new administrators working with city officials, complemented by a modern school building with state-of-the-art shop facilities.

The State Focuses on Springfield

In the early 2000s, state officials were concerned about the high schools in the Springfield school district, according to Kevin McCaskill, a former principal at Putnam Academy. McCaskill became principal in 2004, after spending 18 years in middle school and elementary school administration. At the time of his transfer, Putnam Academy had been labeled "chronically underperforming."[110]

In addition to the abysmal graduation and dropout rates, Putnam Academy's MCAS scores were low, and the school was under-enrolled. It had a capacity for more than 1,000 students but was well under that level. McCaskill understood why enrollment was down.

"(Putnam) was considered almost like a dumping ground," said McCaskill, an experienced middle school teacher and administrator. "It didn't have a good reputation, and you tried to steer kids and families away from Putnam. But there was a lack of understanding about the power of vocational schools."

Identifying the Need for a Turnaround

Putnam Academy was important to Springfield's future because of the skilled workers it could provide to local employers. A failed voc-tech school would be a lost opportunity for the city. Momentum began to build by promoting the Putnam Academy at the middle schools and by strengthening connections with area businesses.

McCaskill said the biggest factor was upgrading the supplemental portion of the school. There was additional emphasis put on after-school programming such as tutorials, clubs, and other extracurricular activities.

"We also made a big effort to get partners," he said. "Between

Springfield College, Amherst College, Mount Holyoke College, we had so many people with their hands on that school to provide holistic support to our students. It was tremendous."

By 2010, the dropout rate, which had been more than 33 percent in 2006, was down to just under 17 percent, although still well above the voc-tech average of 5.9 percent that year.[111] The graduation rate had risen to almost 70 percent, up from 49.2 percent in 2006. Yet that improvement also lagged the 88 percent average graduation rate for all voc-tech schools in the state.

Enrollment climbed from 982 students in the 2003–2004 school year to 1,632 in the 2008–2009 school year.[112] More families were viewing Putnam Academy as an option.

Audit Problems Discovered

McCaskill left Putnam Academy in 2010 for a position with the Hartford Public Schools. He was replaced by Gilbert Traverso, who had spent the previous 14 years as assistant principal of the Connecticut Technical High School system. Traverso conducted a deep review of each vocational department and found problems with many of the shops.

The school's accounting of income from the shops was in disarray. A subsequent audit by Springfield's Office of Internal Audit found "dismal bookkeeping and rampant skimming among a group of employees who used school funds, equipment and student labor for personal home makeovers and sideline businesses."[113]

The abuse was most apparent in Putnam's Automotive Technology and Carpentry programs.

"Educators in both departments pocketed cash and skimmed materials and services for their own use," according to the report.

"There was no effective process for collecting funds for money that the kids made on jobs for the school," said Traverso. "There was a person skimming money from those jobs. There was no evaluation system."[114]

"We didn't have proper structures in place," said McCaskill. "As a practice in all the vocational schools, there's a business manager. We didn't have one at the school. As someone coming to a high school from an elementary school, where you don't deal with those types of funds, I should have had more insight. We didn't have the accountable structures in place."

Massachusetts General Law Chapter 74, which governs the state's voc-tech program, requires schools to have advisory committees for each vocational program. But Traverso found that most programs had no committee or, at best, one that was barely functioning.[115]

Traverso Leads Turnaround Efforts

When Traverso called a first meeting of all advisory committees and vocational chairs, very few showed up. He threatened to stop funding any trade program that did not have an active advisory committee. After that, his meetings had "nothing but perfect attendance with active advisory committees."[116]

As the financial corruption was being addressed, Traverso turned to what he calls "academic corruption" for an underappreciation of how vocational education could change lives. As a youth, he lacked direction until he was admitted into an electrical apprenticeship program.

"That training changed my trajectory, changed my life, and influenced who I am today," he said. "I felt that we needed to go back to the drawing board and start fresh with our teachers. We had some great teachers working in the midst of chaos, controlling their class, building rapports with their students, really taking a wholehearted look at the kids' needs, with little direction. Those are the teachers I started leaning on academically and vocationally for leadership in the building. I had them running meetings, trying to get them to be department chairs. Some were promoted to administration levels as we rebuilt the entire organizational structure."[117]

Traverso implemented a series of programs to strengthen academics. One was called the "Implementation of Sustainable Change." It was made up of four phases: inception, incubation, inclusiveness, and interdependence. Through a flowchart, he showed his staff where the school was in the program in 2010 and where he wanted them all to take it. As they moved through the phases, Traverso and his team made data-driven decisions and analyzed what was working and corrected what was not.

"If we put the systems and structures in place and we all meet and understand the part we play in that, then we all hold each other accountable," he said.

Team meetings were held for each vocational group to determine the school's strengths and weaknesses in critical measurables such as MCAS, attendance, graduation, and internships — and how the problems could be fixed.

To address the school's chronic dropout problem, an early warning system was created, including an array of remediation steps, such as assigning students a dropout coach and a counselor.

New Building, New Attitude

The time spent creating the new advisory boards was valuable, Traverso said, because the industry representatives on each board helped to design the shops for a new building opening in 2012.

Upgrades in technology were occurring so fast that many departments were revised between the initial blueprint and the start of construction. In Graphics, for example, a darkroom was no longer necessary. Additionally, the connections with the advisory boards made possible donations of money, services, and equipment from the business community.

"We had to build those connections to show that we respected their input and their support, and that helped us gain credibility in terms of selling the school," Traverso said.

The opening of the new $114 million school in 2012 provided a powerful boost to the turnaround. It replaced the school's original facility, a New Deal-era Works Project Administration structure built in 1938. The design of the facility was created with input from the advisory boards of each of the 22 shop programs.

Ninety percent of the cost was reimbursed to the city by the Massachusetts School Building Authority. A portion of the new building was similar to a shopping mall in which many of the vocational programs could maintain a storefront to sell their products. It instilled a sense of pride among the staff and students, according to George Johnson, current principal at Putnam Academy and assistant principal in 2012.[118] The momentum that had been building behind Putnam Academy grew.

"We had an admissions policy enacted then on how to get into Putnam, based on certain scores and academics, attendance, recommendations from counselors at the middle school," said Johnson. "Now the high-achieving kids wanted to come to Putnam.

"There were still counselors directing kids somewhere else because in the beginning they were still leery of what Putnam had to offer," he added. "But once we started to do well academically with our MCAS scores and our graduation rate climbing tremendously, people started to take Putnam seriously."

In 2011, the dropout rate had risen to 18.9 percent, but then began to decline sharply, reaching 1.1 percent in 2018. In 2020, it was 2.1 percent.[119] The graduation rate peaked at 99.1 percent in 2017, exceeding the statewide voc-tech average.

MCAS scores also rose sharply beginning in 2012. The percentage of students scoring in the Advanced category reached 7.1 percent, up from the 0.3 percent in 2006. From 2013 through 2018, the school averaged 20.9 percent of students in the Advanced category, peaking at 29.5 percent in 2018. During the same period, 64 percent of the students taking the MCAS exam reached the Proficient level, compared to 22.6 percent in 2006.

A 'Miraculous' Time

Traverso said that to prep for the MCAS exams, five assessment teams were created, each including a math teacher and an ELA teacher. They would work with 22 students per MCAS class and assess their progress on six-week cycles. The data would tell the team leaders where the students needed to be retaught, and they would then share that information with academic teachers.

In 2014, Traverso left Putnam Academy to become the principal at Martha's Vineyard Regional High School. A year later, he took a job with the New Haven, Connecticut school district.

In 2020, he became the director of the Paulo Freire Social Justice Charter School in Chicopee. He calls his time at Putnam Academy "miraculous."

"Given the extent of the problems, I would have to say it took a heck of a lot out of me," he said. "I didn't know the depth of the problems. I had to change belief, and that was hard. All of those gains made the teachers believers, as well as the administrators. The staff contributed to making it what it was."

NEASC Commendations

In December 2014, the New England Association of Schools and Colleges published its Decennial Report on Putnam Academy. It observed that "the atmosphere at PVTA conveys a positive and exciting buzz. Students appear happy to be here and teachers are clearly devoted to their mission."[120]

The review also commended the administration for "the reorganization of administrative structures and the adoption of new policies and practices that assure transparency and honesty in financial administration and expenditure of taxpayer dollars."[121]

Summary

Prior to their turnarounds, Worcester Technical High School and the Roger L. Putnam Vocational Technical Academy ranked near or at the bottom of voc-tech schools in Massachusetts. They were outliers in a system that is highly regarded across the U.S.

The willingness of numerous parties to collaborate in their revivals, including business leaders, city and state officials, parents, and community organizations, indicates how valued these voc-tech schools are to their areas. Companies need a supply of skilled laborers to operate in a community. If that pool of workers is unavailable, employers move elsewhere, and the local economy suffers.

Recommendations

Recruit a business leader to spearhead fundraising

In order to thrive, voc-tech schools need close ties with their business communities. A dynamic business leader who can act as an advocate for the school in the private sector is invaluable for raising money and equipment donations. For Worcester Tech, that man was the late Edwin "Ted" Coghlin, a respected businessman with deep roots in the community.

Don't expect principals to know everything

Upon being named National High School Principal of the Year, Sheila Harrity counseled other principals, especially those new to the job, to recruit people who can help them. Include those who are masters of their trade and teachers who can be empowered to take calculated risks to the benefit of their students and their school.

Highlight the importance of academics to vocational skills

Both Harrity and Traverso believe that the link between academics and vocational skills should be more emphasized. Traverso talks about how closer attention to algebra lessons in high school would have helped him years later as an electrical contractor when trying to figure the circumference of a swimming pool.

Establish a dedicated fund

Unlike regional voc-tech schools that serve a group of communities and are governed by a district school committee made up of representatives from the member communities, Worcester Tech and Putnam Academy are part of their city's school system. To afford a major transformation, additional funds are needed, typically in the form of a 501(c)(3) nonprofit.

In Worcester, the Skyline Technical Fund helped finance the purchase of computers and related equipment. Putnam Academy has the Putnam Technical Fund, which supports "current and future training courses" at the school and can be used to solicit contributions for the benefit of students, faculty, and programs.[122]

■ ■ ■

William Donovan is a former staff writer with the Providence Journal in Rhode Island, where he wrote about business and government. He has taught business journalism in the graduate programs at Boston University and Northeastern University. He received his undergraduate degree from Boston College and his master's degree in Journalism from American University in Washington, D.C.

Chapter 7

Expanding Access to Vocational-Technical Education in Massachusetts

by Ken Ardon and Alison L. Fraser

It is clear from assessment, graduation, and follow-up data that career voc-tech education in Massachusetts is a success. Although it is acknowledged that college is not the path for every high school graduate, voc-tech high schools make sure that every student is prepared for college, has the choice between college and career, and that that option is not taken away because of lack of preparation.

Voc-tech education has come into its own. Families across the Commonwealth are appreciating the relevance and rigor inherent in completing a full academic schedule every other week, alternating with the in-depth study of a trade or career of their student's choice.

As this chapter explores, voc-tech education is so popular that there are now about 5,000 more applicants for places in Massachusetts's voc-tech schools than there are openings. Parents recognize that the discipline needed to complete a Department of Elementary and Secondary Education (DESE) standards-based curriculum and achieve industry-recognized credentials in a career tech program is an excellent way to prepare for a successful life.

According to a statewide survey of business owners and others by the Dukakis Center at Northeastern University, vocational school graduates are more job-ready than general education or college preparatory high school graduates. Some respondents felt that voc-tech graduates were often more job-ready than even *college* graduates.

Employers at a 2015 Worcester County Chamber of Commerce Manufacturing Roundtable agreed that voc-tech graduates are often more team-oriented, disciplined, and prepared to enter the workforce. These elements have combined to create a need for more access to Chapter 74 certified voc-tech education.

This chapter examines:

- The conditions that have brought us to the present predicament whereby we have waiting lists for vocational education
- Why 52 Massachusetts cities and towns do not have access to either district or regional voc-tech programs
- Funding for voc-tech education, including the fact that 5,000 more voc-tech placements could be created for less than one-half of 1 percent of the state's FY16 education budget

Introduction

Career voc-tech education has a successful history in Massachusetts.[123] Each year, voc-tech schools provide tens of thousands of students with both a traditional Massachusetts academic standards-based high school education and applied training in a variety of programs that gives them an excellent opportunity to find skilled, high-wage careers.

Voc-tech schools—and regional voc-tech schools in particular—do an excellent job teaching traditional academic subjects. They have lower dropout rates than traditional high schools, as well as strong attendance and performance on MCAS, and a high percentage of graduates who go on to postsecondary institutions.[124]

Yet many voc-tech schools do not have the capacity to accommodate all students who apply. For many years, political leaders have touted the benefits of voc-tech education, but programs have not expanded, and waitlists remain.

The primary factor limiting the expansion of voc-tech schools is how they are financed. Voc-tech schools are by their nature more expensive than traditional schools, and regional voc-tech schools compete with other local and district schools for funding.

Many years ago, Massachusetts provided incentives for regionalization that encouraged municipalities to join regional voc-tech districts, but these incentives have long since been eliminated.

Background: Vocational-Technical Education in Massachusetts

Students and their families have several options for school choice in Massachusetts. The two major options beyond local district schools are charter public schools, which enroll more than 47,000 students, and voc-tech programs, which enroll more than 52,600.

The voc-tech options include regional voc-tech school districts as well as independent voc-tech schools and comprehensive schools that offer some vocational programs. All such programs must meet the requirements of Chapter 74 of the Massachusetts General Laws and be approved by the DESE.

There are an additional 9,140 students in programs that meet the federal Perkins Act definition of career and technical education but are not approved under Chapter 74 — meaning that they have not completed the rigorous two-year DESE protocol for earning an approved Classification of Instructional Programs (CIP) code.

For many families, a voc-tech education may be their only alternative to the traditional local school. This could occur if there are no charter public schools nearby, a distinct possibility given that 75 percent of the state's charter schools are in urban areas.[125]

Even if there is a charter school in an area, families with older students may not have access to them. Forty-four percent of charter schools serve students only up to middle school, and 75 percent of the charter schools that serve high school students start accepting students at lower grades (i.e., they serve grades 6–12 or K–12).

These factors leave few slots open at charter schools for older students and leave many families with no real alternative to their local district school. While voc-tech schools offer choice to many families, students are not always free to apply to the programs they choose.

Voc-Tech Enrollment and Demand in Massachusetts

Chapter 74 voc-tech programs	52,600
Perkins Act CVTE programs	9,140
Students on waiting lists	5,000+

Source: Massachusetts Department of Elementary and Secondary Education

For example, if a student lives in a city or town that offers one or more voc-tech programs at its local district high school, the student may be unable to attend neighboring regional voc-tech schools. The local program prevents that student from accessing what are often more extensive and better-equipped offerings at the nearly regional voc-tech school.

Massachusetts has 45 approved occupational programs, ranging from agriculture to telecommunications. Many programs have remained popular over time, although the top four programs enroll fewer students than they did in the past—just over 10,700—as enrollment has spread more evenly across the dozens of other programs offered.

Many voc-tech programs have proven very popular in Massachusetts, particularly at regional vocational schools. According to DESE data, 18 percent of Massachusetts students in grades 9–12 are enrolled in a vocational program, and surveys and reports consistently show that voc-tech schools throughout the Commonwealth have long waiting lists.

Waiting lists tend to be longest in districts serving at-risk populations, such as low-income students and students whose first language is not English. The high numbers of applications exceeding available seats — sometimes as many as two for every opening — at many regional voc-tech schools clearly indicate that parents believe in the schools.

According to October 2015 DESE data, regional voc-tech schools had better attendance rates and lower dropout rates than traditional high schools, despite having a higher share of low-income students: 44 percent in regional vocational schools compared to 39 percent statewide.

And DESE data from 2021–2022 showed that voc-tech schools' edge in attendance and dropout rates was achieved despite having a higher share of students with disabilities — 24 percent — versus the 19 percent at schools statewide.

In fact, their success is particularly striking among low-income students. At the same time, student performance on the MCAS roughly matches the statewide averages.

While the performance of regional voc-tech students has been impressive, direct comparisons of student achievement are difficult because vocational schools with more applicants than available spaces can assess prospective students on attendance, behavior, and vocational interest, using admissions plans developed in concert with DESE regulations.

Enrollment Patterns in Vocational and Traditional Schools

Altogether, Chapter 74 voc-tech programs enroll almost 52,600 students in grades 9–12. The popularity of voc-tech education varies around the state. Excluding Nantucket and Martha's Vineyard, enrollment ranges from a low of approximately 6 percent in Suffolk County to a high of approximately 32 percent in Bristol County.

The state's counties also vary widely in the share of vocational students attending regional schools. While regional schools account for roughly 60 percent of overall vocational enrollment, the shares range from less than 10 percent in Dukes and Hampden counties to more than 75 percent in Middlesex and Barnstable counties and 100 percent in Franklin County.

The enrollment by county data show very low overall vocational enrollment in Suffolk County, which is driven mostly by Boston. This suggests that vocational enrollment in urban centers might be lower than in other areas.

---

52 cities and towns in Massachusetts are not members of a regional vocational district and do not offer vocational programs at the local or regional high school level. These municipalities serve more than 13,000 high school students.

However, the municipal districts in the 10 largest cities in the state send a higher percentage of students to vocational programs than the overall state average: 22 percent in these cities compared to 15 percent in other areas. These cities also have many more students in vocational programs that have not been approved under Chapter 74 — an additional 4,200 students are enrolled in these programs, nearly three times the percentage in other areas.

While these cities send many students to vocational programs, the figures vary tremendously. Boston stands out on the low end, enrolling only about 6 percent of its students in local voc-tech programs, with another 6 percent at non-Chapter 74 programs. On the other end of the spectrum, more than one-quarter of the students in Worcester and Cambridge attend local vocational programs, while in Quincy the figure is almost half.

Several cities also send large numbers of students to regional schools. For example, New Bedford, which has only one local Chapter 74 program, sends 1,700 students to the Greater New Bedford Regional Vocational Technical School District.

Many areas are served by more than one voc-tech program.

Regional voc-tech schools serve 240 municipalities. The regional membership overlaps almost entirely with the county agricultural schools, which serve 48 cities and towns; the two systems together serve a total of 246 municipalities.

At the same time, 38 local districts have local voc-tech programs, and 23 of those are in municipalities that are not members of either the regional or county districts. Finally, 12 regional high schools also have voc-tech programs — these schools serve 37 cities and towns, 30 of which are not in other systems.

In total, 299 municipalities around the Commonwealth have direct access to vocational education through regional voc-techs, county agricultural schools, local vocational schools or programs, or a program within a regional district.

This leaves 52 cities and towns that are not members of a regional vocational district and do not offer vocational programs at the local or regional high school level. These municipalities serve roughly 45,000 students, including more than 13,000 high school students.

The majority of these towns — 32 of 52 — are in Berkshire and Hampshire counties. Many students in Middlesex, Plymouth, and Worcester counties are also in this situation. These figures refer to voc-tech programs approved under Chapter 74; some of these areas have career and technical education programs that were not approved under Chapter 74.

Overall statewide high school enrollments fell significantly between 2005 and 2015, then stabilized and have remained relatively steady over the last several years. Overall, for the period from 2012 to 2021, enrollment statement was by about 41,840 students, or 4.4 percent.[126]

The decline in enrollment was particularly severe in western Massachusetts, but almost every part of the state has lost students. Yet, despite the declines, enrollment at vocational schools has grown by more than 7,850 students, or 17.6 percent, during these years.

That increased enrollment took place in all types of vocational schools — enrollment in regional vocational schools increased by 2,700 and enrollment in other vocational programs increased by 2,642.

Enrollment growth in vocational programs was particularly strong in Bristol and Worcester counties, growing by almost 2,000 students in each region. At the same time, vocational enrollment fell in Suffolk and Berkshire counties.

While regional vocational schools have grown an average of 10.5 percent, some schools have seen rapid enrollment growth and others have seen modest declines.

The fastest expansion came in Worcester County, where Assabet Valley, Blackstone Valley Tech, and Bay Path (Southern Worcester) all expanded, and total enrollment grew by 21 percent. Similarly, the five schools in Bristol County had combined growth of 860 students. There are a handful of regional schools that saw enrollment decline, most severely at Cape Cod Tech and Minuteman Tech.

Although many vocational schools have expanded in the past decade, vocational programs still have substantial waiting lists. As stated previously, the total number of students waiting for spots in recent years was at least 4,400 and probably much higher. It would require a substantial expansion of vocational programs to satisfy this demand.

Vocational School Finance

The financial impact of an expansion of vocational education in Massachusetts is determined by the school finance system. As with all schools, vocational schools are financed by a combination of local and state funding.

State aid to fund operating expenses is governed primarily by the Chapter 70 funding formula, while state aid for capital expenditures on new construction or substantial repair or renovation of existing facilities is provided by the Massachusetts School Building Authority (MSBA).

Vocational programs are more expensive to operate than traditional schools because they must offer both academic classroom instruction as well as certified instruction in specific vocational fields. The costs of vocational programs vary, but all require additional resources beyond a traditional high school. And these schools must adapt to changes in technology and workforce needs more quickly than traditional schools.

In FY2020, regional vocational schools spent roughly $22,400 per student,[127] compared to average spending in other schools of $17,131 and a statewide average of $17,575.

However, it is not appropriate to compare vocational schools to these averages, for several reasons. The traditional school averages include elementary and middle schools, which are generally less expensive to operate than high schools. At the same time, the other averages also include some vocational programs within districts, which muddies the comparison.

An accurate assessment would compare the cost of a vocational program to the cost of the traditional high school program that a student would otherwise have attended. However, this comparison is difficult because expenditure data is more easily compared across districts rather than schools.

To avoid this complication, one way to gauge the extra cost of vocational education is to compare regional vocational schools with regional high schools.

Not surprisingly, regional vocational schools spend more per pupil than regional high schools. The difference is smaller than the $6,000 difference between regional vocational schools and the state average, but it is significant. Some of the largest differences, as might be expected, are in classroom specialists, equipment and technology, and operations and maintenance.

The differences in instructional spending are not driven by higher teacher salaries at regional vocational schools, which are only marginally above the state average. Rather, regional voc-tech students complete two programs, with the necessary extra human capital needed for instruction.

The Chapter 70 aid formula recognizes the extra expense of voc-tech education in the calculation of the foundation budget, which measures the minimum required spending level in each district. The formula adjusts the foundation budget upwards by roughly $5,000 in vocational schools.

There are many other factors in the formula, such as the number of low-income students or English Language Learners, so that the foundation budget varies across vocational schools. However, the general pattern is that vocational schools are expected to spend substantially more than other schools.

Chapter 70 not only calculates the minimum spending necessary in each district, but it also determines how much state aid districts receive. Because the Chapter 70 formula is very complex, the results vary for each district and for each town that is a member of a regional district. However, the higher foundation budget in vocational schools and districts means that, all else being equal, the state will often contribute more aid toward the cost of career voc-tech high schools.

The differences across regional schools get wider when the regional members are examined individually; the required local contribution for separate municipal members of a regional district often vary significantly. The figures for expenditures per pupil and required spending suggest that the extra cost of vocational education is somewhere around $5,000 per student.

This additional cost means that significant expansion of vocational education would require additional funding, but the expense would represent less than one half of one percent of the Commonwealth's annual education budget.

Adding space for 5,000 students — enough to roughly eliminate the known waiting lists — could cost $20 million per year before considering capital costs, which are discussed below. The precise number depends on many factors, including which vocational programs are expanded and where the expansion takes place.

The location of expansion also has a large impact on who would pay for the additional spaces. The large differences in state aid and required contribution across districts and member communities means that the burden depends on where the new students come from. To simplify, expansion in high-income or property-rich areas would impose higher costs on local communities, while if new students came from less affluent areas, the state would cover a greater share of the costs.

Capital Costs

In addition to annual operating costs, vocational schools also face substantial costs for facilities and capital equipment. Any large expansion of vocational schools would require new construction or significant renovation of existing facilities.

As with traditional schools, vocational schools are eligible for funding through the Massachusetts School Building Authority. When a project is approved, MSBA provides a reimbursement rate that covers a portion of eligible costs, and the rate depends on community income, poverty, and property wealth, as well as incentive points based on construction choices.[128]

Vocational schools' requirements for larger workspaces and equipment mean that capital costs are higher than in traditional schools. According to the most recent needs survey from the MSBA, in 2016 the average vocational school was 39 percent larger than a traditional high school.[129]

The survey also noted that "Vocational Technical High Schools may require more thoughtful design of acoustical elements and building systems, particularly electrical, plumbing and ventilation, in order to support the vocational program and ensure a safe and healthy physical environment."

In the past, the state provided more generous reimbursement to regional districts, as well as additional aid to cover transportation costs.[130] When this regional aid was phased out in the 1990s, it reduced the incentive for regional members to agree to renovation or new construction.

Most regional voc-tech schools were built in the late 1960s and early 1970s, while schools in Bristol and Norfolk counties are a century old. In 2010, the MSBA rated the building conditions in vocational schools as marginally worse than other schools. While several have had renovations or been rebuilt since then, many vocational buildings require significant work.

The MSBA application process requires support from local

communities. Regional vocational schools must therefore gather support from many member communities, which may be more difficult than for a vocational school within a municipal district that serves just one community.

The process becomes even more problematic for regional schools that enroll a large number of students from non-member cities and towns. The non-member municipalities do not contribute toward capital costs, meaning that member towns must shoulder all expenses not reimbursed by MSBA.

Construction costs vary by community and are subject to many factors, making it difficult to calculate per-pupil costs and limiting the value of such calculations. One factor that may help defray costs, however, is an MSBA estimate — as of 2010 — that Massachusetts has more than one million square feet of unused classroom space. Moreover, the MSBA found that more than 20 percent of schools were larger than their enrollment or education programs required.

The state's 2016 needs survey found a 36 percent increase in underutilized schools in the Commonwealth, and because of the continued population decline since, that percent has continued to grow. But, in another testimony to the growing popularity of voc-tech schools, the three schools in the MSBA pipeline — Northeast Metropolitan, Diman Regional, and Bristol-Plymouth — were expanding to accommodate increased demand and reduce waiting lists.

Just as with operating expenses, the burden of expanding vocational education will shift depending on where the expansion takes place. The minimum reimbursement rate under MSBA is 31 percent, but most districts receive at least 40 percent. In poorer communities the reimbursement rate could be as high as 80 percent, shifting most of the cost to the state.

Conclusion: Opportunities and Challenges
Recommendations:

- Undertake targeted expansion of career voc-tech education modeled on successful independent regional programs

- Focus on geographical areas not currently served by existing career voc-tech schools and areas where applications greatly exceed available student spots
- Provide Massachusetts School Building Authority incentives for projects that reduce waiting lists and projects that repurpose existing space

The success of vocational education in Massachusetts provides an opportunity. Expanded access to vocational education could benefit thousands of students, particularly students who are not well served in traditional schools. Vocational programs provide excellent career training, as well as the traditional academic education required to attend college. Of course, not all vocational education programs are created equal, and any expansion should focus on the features of the regional programs that have proven most successful.

While expanding career voc-tech education comes with a potentially significant price tag, it also carries great value for its graduates—both a high school diploma and a competency determination in the student's career technical program, along with third-party certifications, such as from OSHA, SolidWorks, or the EPA.

Beyond the perennial debates over school expansion and funding, the debate over the value of voc-tech schools has been put to rest by decades of clear achievements.

Students who succeed at career voc-tech schools are:
- Far less likely to drop out of school
- Far more likely to contribute to Massachusetts's economy
- Better prepared than many regular high school graduates to fill job openings
- Earn higher wages and pay more in taxes
- Require fewer public benefits

The success of many career voc-tech education programs strongly suggests that expanding these opportunities would be a wise investment for the Commonwealth.

■ ■ ■

Ken Ardon, Ph.D., is a professor of economics at Salem State University, where he has taught since 2004, as well as a member of Pioneer Institute's Center for School Reform Advisory Board. He received a Ph.D. in Economics from the University of California at Santa Barbara in 1999, where he co-authored a book on school spending and student achievement. He taught economics at Pomona College before moving to Massachusetts. From 2000 to 2004, Dr. Ardon worked for the Commonwealth of Massachusetts in the Executive Office of Administration and Finance.

Alison L. Fraser is an education policy, research, and strategy consultant and president of Practical Policy. Previously, she was an administrator at Blackstone Valley Tech and director of policy and advocacy at Mass Insight Education, where she directed the Great Schools Campaign and development of No Excuses for Failing Schools and Excellence in Math and Science Goals. An expert in standards-based curriculum, Fraser has coordinated activities and programs for the Coalition for Higher Standards and led research in standards-based reform.

Chapter 8

Voc-Tech in Massachusetts: Remaining True to Founding Principles

by Wilfrid J. Savoie

In 1906, the Commonwealth of Massachusetts, long known as a pioneer in public education, industry, and the humanities, became the first state in the Union to offer public vocational-technical education to its youth.

More than a century later, the state continues to demonstrate that its unique combination of high academic expectations and professional-level occupational training is a resounding success.

In this concluding chapter, we explore further some of the reasons that Massachusetts has long been a model of voc-tech education for the nation.

The factors that gave rise to the first generation of voc-tech and agricultural schools are rooted deeply in the state's history and geography. Those schools were founded in the early twentieth century.

Next, following World War II, a "perfect storm" of economic, social, and cultural forces helped spur the establishment, growth, and expansion of a second generation of schools that featured regional voc-tech districts.

Finally, in the years since the landmark 1993 Massachusetts Education Reform Act, the state's voc-tech community has once again demonstrated its remarkable ability to adapt to changing times, re-envisioning voc-tech education through what constitutes a third generation of schools.

Initial resistance to higher academic standards quickly gave way to the recognition of the growing importance of the academic side of vocational education—a natural development accompanying the rise of the Computer and Information ages.

Today, voc-tech schools across Massachusetts can point to stellar graduation rates, minuscule dropout rates, and an enviable record of placing their graduates in the widest possible variety of postsecondary roles—from traditional trades and increasingly sophisticated high-tech careers to colleges and universities, training programs, and military service.

Notably, voc-tech schools have achieved these successes even as they enroll, on average, higher percentages of low-income and special needs students than traditional academic public schools.

But perhaps the most remarkable aspect of voc-tech's Massachusetts success story is that these schools have progressed into the twenty-first century while remaining true to the vision that gave birth to them in the much simpler times of 1906.

That fact alone speaks to strength and wisdom of their founding principles—and is perhaps the most eloquent argument for remaining true to those principles during an age when educational theories and fads abound.

I: 1906 Origins: 'Practicality and Relevance' Give Rise to Industrial Schools

In retrospect, William Lewis Douglas seems to have been destined to found voc-tech education in Massachusetts. Born in Plymouth, he began working at age seven, served in the Civil War, and founded a shoe manufacturing business in Brockton that grew into one of the largest such enterprises in the world.

During his one year in the state's highest office, Governor Douglas recommended the creation of a Commission on Industrial and Technical Education to investigate the need for education in the skill areas that would support the industries of the Commonwealth.

In April 1906, the Douglas Commission report thoroughly crystallized the industrial education movement in arriving at two major conclusions.

- First, noting the need for an alternative form of education that was practical and relevant to the real world, the report declared: "For the great majority of children who leave school to enter employment... (these children) would be attracted to further school training of a practical character..."[131]
- Second, the authors recognized that economic growth and prosperity are dependent upon an educated and skilled workforce: "In the long run that industry, wherever in the world it is located, which combines with general intelligence the broadest technical knowledge and the highest technical skill, will command the markets of the world."[132]
- The Douglas Commission also recognized the necessity for the Commonwealth to adequately fund vocational education, noting that "Whatever may be the cost of such training, the failure to furnish it would in the end be more costly."[133]

Commission on Industrial Education Founded

Legislation was enacted in June 1906 to establish the Commission on Industrial Education, which was responsible for the establishment and oversight of industrial schools, for both boys and girls, that were to run parallel to and independent of the public school system.

These first industrial schools offered programs in trades and industries, household arts, and agriculture — for both youth and adults — with both day and evening classes.

In 1909, political pressure and urging from the educational field eventually resulted in the Commission on Industrial Education and the Board of Education being consolidated into one agency, thereby creating one educational system under a new Board of Education.

In becoming the first state to publicly found industrial schools, Massachusetts became a model for other states and a blueprint for the federal Smith-Hughes National Vocational

Education Act of 1917.

And nowhere did industrial schools take hold as they did in the Commonwealth. Spurred by the demands for practical training that accompanied two world wars and the Great Depression, the schools grew rapidly. By 1960, Massachusetts had 56 trade and vocational schools for boys, six for girls, and three county agricultural schools — serving 13,466 students.[134]

II: A Midcentury Encore of 'Second-Generation' Schools

By the middle of the twentieth century, voc-tech education in Massachusetts could look back on some 50 years of success in training generations of skilled workers — auto mechanics, plumbers, electricians, machinists, farmers, hairdressers, cooks, and homemakers.

But a growing population of Baby Boomers and the first stirrings of the high-technology industries that would become the foundation of the "Massachusetts Miracle" placed major demands on public education in the state.

First, state officials, educators and the public recognized the need for more schools and more sophisticated offerings to keep pace with a changing economy.

Second, superintendents began to be concerned about where they would house growing numbers of elementary and secondary school students.

Regionalization Meets Voc-Tech Education

A third factor was also in play. In the light of changing economic and demographic factors educational attitudes began to change in many Massachusetts communities in the 1940s. Where it had historically been very difficult to bring cities and towns together for educational purposes — apart from county agricultural schools — many now perceived advantages in regionalization.

In 1948, a special state commission recommended the establishment of regional high school districts, citing the opportunity to offer a greater variety of programs, including vocational subjects. A year later, the first laws governing regional school districts were enacted.

1955 and Beyond: The First Regional High Schools Open

Silver Lake Regional High School, which included a vocational component, opened in September 1955 to serve the towns of Kingston, Plympton, and Halifax.

The next two decades saw a building boom as one regional district after another was established. The second regional school to include vocational programs, King Philip Regional High School in Wrentham, was established in 1957. Dighton-Rehoboth Regional High School in North Dighton followed in 1961.

As voc-tech education in Massachusetts came of age through the last half of the twentieth century, it remained true to a tradition that has long emphasized practical skills and a focus on the economic value of education to students and businesses.

Surveys conducted between 1960 and 1963 considered the construction of one or more schools in many regions throughout the state.[135] The state Department of Education's 1962 Annual Report focused on city trade schools that had had to limit enrollment by nonresidents in the face of increasing suburban populations that wanted access to vocational schools.

Walter J. Markham, the state's director of vocational education from 1954 until 1970, took a new approach, stressing quality vocational education, with more diversified training, to significant numbers of students at an affordable cost to communities.

Between 1962 and 1978, 27 vocational schools were established to directly serve two-third of Massachusetts's 351 cities and towns — and help supply workers to industries.

The Cold War and 1958's National Defense Education Act

International events also spurred the growth of voc-tech in Massachusetts.

In the wake of the Soviet Union's October 1957 launch of *Sputnik 1*, the first artificial Earth satellite, Congress passed the National Defense Education Act (NDEA), signed into law by President Eisenhower on September 2, 1958.

That legislation provided funding to improve American schools and promote education beyond high school. The NDEA's Title VIII section made voc-tech programs available to residents in inadequately served areas. Federal aid covered equipment, materials, and salaries for voc-tech training of youth and adults in scientific and technical fields that met national defense needs.[136]

Massachusetts took advantage by identifying existing programs that would qualify for federal funding and establishing new technical courses that would meet Title VIII requirements.

1963 Legislation Gives Rise to Second-Generation Schools

In October 1961, President Kennedy established a panel to evaluate federal vocational education laws. Their recommendations led to Congress giving overwhelming support to the Vocational Education Act of 1963, which provided grants for states to maintain, improve, and further develop voc-tech programs at the high school and postsecondary levels.

Federal funding for voc-tech education was increased to $279 million, five times what had been authorized by the Smith-Hughes National Vocational Education Act of 1917 and reauthorized in 1956. The law also amended and extended the NDEA for three years.[137]

In Massachusetts, regional school districts had new financial incentives for construction and expansion of a second generation of voc-tech schools.

Expanding Voc-Tech Opportunities for All

It was during these "second generation" years that voc-tech education acquired many of the characteristics it retains today. A 1968 amendment to the 1963 law made specific reference to students with special needs, and a 1976 amendment promoted equal opportunities for women and girls.

Schools throughout Massachusetts improved access for handicapped, at-risk, and adult populations and addressed the challenges of sex and gender bias.

The 1984 and succeeding vocational legislative acts were named for the late Rep. Carl D. Perkins, a Kentucky Democrat, who had long been a champion of vocational education.

The acts promoted funding for students with special needs, greater accountability, secondary-postsecondary alignment, academic integration, tech prep, and business partnerships. The 2006 legislation, known as Perkins IV, dropped the term "vocational education" in favor of "career technical education."

The latest reauthorization, Perkins V, came in 2018 and provided $1.2 billion to support career and technical education and provide increased flexibility for states.

Massachusetts Focuses on 'Economic Independence'

As voc-tech education in Massachusetts came of age through the last half of the twentieth century, it remained true to a tradition that has long emphasized practical skills and a focus on the economic value of education to students and businesses.

Annual federal funding for vocational education to Massachusetts in recent years has been approximately $20 million. While modest, that funding, with various priorities and set-asides, has had a significant impact on the state's career voc-tech and agricultural programs.

Still, because of key differences as to what kind of programming qualifies for federal Perkins funding and what meets Massachusetts's Chapter 74 requirements, the Commonwealth remained focused on a voc-tech system that prepares students for "economic independence" as part of an educated and skilled workforce.

More evolution was to come with the passage of the Massachusetts Education Reform Act. But to better understand the impact and importance of the MERA and the recent history of voc-tech education in Massachusetts, we first revisit voc-tech's unique instructional methodology and its relationship with the business community.

III. The Evolution of a Unique Instructional Methodology

To casual observers, it may seem that today's voc-tech schools are simply more sophisticated versions of their counterparts from a century ago, featuring advanced machinery, gleaming new buildings, and ubiquitous computers.

A closer look suggests that first-generation industrial schools and second-generation voc-tech schools differed greatly in their approach to developing core academic skills. How that change took place is crucial for understanding the advances voc-tech education has made. And how administrators and staff handle academics will be critical in the decades ahead.

The Broadening Role of Academics

Initially, all academic instruction had to be directly applied to a trade. The early industrial schools never dismissed the value of reading and mathematics, but those skills were valued primarily for their application to the practical skills that were the primary order of business.

The rise of second-generation schools in the 1940s and 1950s, however, brought a change. Rising expectations, increasing technical sophistication in all fields, and the demands of high school accreditation combined to push voc-tech schools toward an embrace of academics with less direct application to any specific area of study.

This trend continued into the 1990s, when the purpose of voc-tech education expanded still further to become a dual mission of preparing students for both gainful employment and postsecondary education, whether that meant attending a four-year college or obtaining certifications and additional expertise through training programs and institutes for career purposes.

Whatever graduates' career paths, voc-tech leaders came to realize that the scope and rigor of the academic courses they offer must match that of traditional high schools.

The Constant Factor: The Integrity of Intensive Skill Training

The expanding and changing role of academics in voc-tech education must also be viewed against a backdrop of remarkable consistency and stability in the core mission of these schools — vocational training.

Both first-generation industrial trade schools and second-generation voc-tech schools were structured and characterized by their distinctive form of project-based instructional methodology, real-world curriculum, and industry-standard facilities and equipment.

Whatever other factors have been at play over time, voc-tech schools have always borne in mind that their primary mission remains the training of students to become valuable members of the local, regional, and state workforces. And achieving that task means, above all, ensuring that voc-tech students have sufficient time on task to acquire the technical skills and knowledge they need.

The Challenge of Education Reform

In light of that core mission, the 1993 Massachusetts Education Reform Act posed a significant challenge to voc-tech schools.

The Act brought new and necessary attention to academic instruction in today's highly technical job market. However, to provide flexibility for additional core academics, the Act also meant a shift in vocational "time on task" — away from a quantitative approach of having one-half of a student's hours devoted to their trade without interruption to a more outcome-oriented approach.

In addition, voc-tech schools since 1993 have embraced industry credentialing to validate the integrity of the technical skills and knowledge they teach. Indeed, such credentialing is now viewed as the gold standard that graduates should meet, and a key measure for gauging the success of the new pedagogical strategies implemented as part of education reform.

For today's third-generation, post-1993 voc-tech schools, the challenge is to fulfill their traditional vocational goals while meeting the newer, higher academic standards. The organization and scheduling challenges are significant, but evidence to date suggests these schools have more than met that challenge.

They have done so in large part by holding true to the principles that have always set them apart, including:

- Prioritizing project-based instructional methodologies
- Aligning curriculum with real-world needs
- Maintaining industry-standard facilities
- Integrating rigorous core academic skills with high-wage technical skills

IV: A Century of Ties to the Business and Labor Communities

To understand the long and intimate connection between voc-tech education and the state's business community, it is helpful to explore some of the history of Worcester between the late nineteenth and early twentieth centuries.

On June 24, 1898, ceremonies at Worcester's Mechanics Hall marked the fiftieth anniversary of the city's incorporation. Among the speakers that Friday evening was Superior Court Judge Frank P. Goulding, who pointed to the city's business community as a key to its past and its future.

"The honor of founding Worcester anew must be accorded to the mechanics and artisans, the manufacturers and businessmen of that generation," Goulding said, alluding to the industrial pioneers of the 1830s, who had built a community on the production of machinery and wire, boots and hats, and coaches and cotton goods.

"The first quality that attracts attention as we try to reproduce in our study of imagination their form and pressure," Goulding continued, "is their practical business sense and sagacity. First of all, they knew how to accomplish a concrete result by conformable concrete means."[138]

Milton Higgins and the Birth of Industrial Schools

The Worcester of 1898 did not yet have an industrial school for its youth, but since its founding in 1865, Worcester Polytechnic Institute had produced graduates "who annually by the score take places of responsibility in our great work-shops, for which they have been so admirably trained."[139]

The driving force behind vocational education in the city had long been Milton P. Higgins, who served as superintendent of the Washburn Shops at WPI from 1868 until January 1896.[140]

Higgins maintained close ties with the city's business community and trained students in manufacturing techniques for products such as lathes, machine tools, and drafting tables. Following his years at WPI, Higgins became Worcester's leading industrialist, devoting his time to the founding and development of major area employers—including the Plunger Elevator Company, Norton Company, and Norton Emery Wheel Company.

Higgins also focused on the training and education of successive generations of students and workers. At a July 1900 meeting of the Society for the Promotion of Engineering Education, held in New York City, Higgins advanced the idea of a self-supporting trade school in which boys would spend half their day in classes and half their day in shop—the same approach he had used at WPI, and which would be the hallmark of voc-tech schools for a century and more to come.

Later, as a member of the Massachusetts Commission on Industrial Education and the Worcester Industrial School Commission, Higgins played a leading role in the establishment of Worcester Boys' Trade in 1910 as the fourth independent industrial school in Massachusetts.

Following Higgins's death in 1912, the school's assembly

room was named Higgins Hall in honor of the man who is today considered the father of the public trade school movement in America.

The Vital Role of Advisory Committees

The 1911 legislation governing industrial schools required the appointment of advisory committees composed of individuals representing local trades, industries, and occupations. Committee members accepted responsibility for the success of a vocational school and were expected to maintain close contact with these institutions and obtain accurate knowledge of their operations.

That pattern has endured in Massachusetts for more than a century.

As potential employers of skilled graduates, businesses have always had an obvious interest in ensuring the quality and success of voc-tech schools. Just as importantly, the experience, expertise, and perspectives of advisory committee members are the most direct means by which voc-tech schools ensure their curriculum remains relevant.

As occupations and industries change, voc-tech administrators, staff, and students know that district and regional school committees have advisors who can point them in the right direction with regard to new equipment, techniques, and technologies.

Today, each voc-tech school has an advisory committee of between 10 and 15 business and community leaders, as well as additional advisory committees for each program. Their work includes ensuring that programs feature state-of-the-art instruction, maintaining the relevance of the curriculum, helping superintendents accurately forecast capital equipment needs, and fostering closer ties with the business community.

Flexible, Effective, and Results-Oriented

Because voc-tech schools focus on training students to meet the needs of employers, they must be able to react more quickly to workforce and technological changes than traditional high schools do. The schools' advisory committees are crucial for that process. They also illustrate the importance of protecting school autonomy over curriculum in voc-tech education.

Advisory committees also foster co-op programs in which qualified seniors spend what would otherwise be their shop weeks working and earning money at a job in their field of study. Those co-ops strengthen the ties voc-techs enjoy with their communities, with many co-op student workers moving directly into full-time positions following graduation.

In addition, voc-tech schools build community ties by opening certain of their facilities to the public on a regular basis, including auto body and repair facilities, restaurants, and cosmetology shops.

Continuity Over a Century

In 2006 — exactly a century after the state authorized the first industrial schools — local Worcester area businesses came together to help fund a new, state-of-the-art campus for the city's nearly century-old trade school.

Led by Edwin "Ted" Coghlin, chairman of both Coghlin Electric and the Worcester Technical High School Board of Trustees, the fundraising included $3 million that was leveraged into a $30 million fund to purchase the latest computer and information technology equipment.

The effort transformed the school. Between the 2003–2004 and 2012–2013 school years, Worcester Tech's dropout rate declined to the lowest among the city's seven high schools.

The Worcester example captures the symbiotic relationship between Massachusetts voc-tech high schools and local businesses, and the benefits of those ties were highlighted in a 2006 report issued by the Massachusetts Business Alliance for Education, "*Employer Perspectives on Work Readiness Skills.*"[141]

The report found general agreement among dozens of participating professionals that "vocational school graduates are more job-ready than general education and college preparatory high school graduates. In fact, a number of participants felt that vocational high school graduates were often more job-ready than college graduates."

Worcester Tech is hardly the only voc-tech success story. When area machine shops were becoming reluctant to hire Franklin County Technical School graduates because the 1940s-vintage mills and lathes they were using in the shops meant retraining students on modern equipment, a coalition of school advisors and community leaders, including 14 businesses, raised over $700,000 to reequip the program.

Responding to a cluster of airports, manufacturers, aircraft service centers, and flight schools in the Pioneer Valley, local companies and the Commonwealth worked with Westfield Technical Academy to start the first aviation technology program in Massachusetts. Students take their academic courses at the school, while hands-on engine, electronics, and body work are taught in a renovated hangar at Westfield-Barnes Airport.

V. The 1993 Education Reform Act

The Massachusetts Education Reform Act of 1993 marked a watershed moment in the history of education in the Commonwealth. Notably, the MERA authorized charter public schools, which have grown to become an important part of the state's public education landscape.

The MERA also ratcheted up academic rigor at voc-tech schools while simultaneously protecting the integrity of intensive skills training. Given increasing workplace demands for both academic and technical skills, it required that voc-tech students, like their counterparts in other high schools, would have to pass MCAS tests to earn a high school degree.

The initial reaction to higher academic standards, including the MCAS requirement, had been mixed. Some in the voc-tech community argued that their students should not be judged by MCAS but should have an equally rigorous measure—a Certificate of Occupational Proficiency—focused on vocational curriculum and achievement.

Test data from the first few years following enactment of the

MERA seemed to justify such concerns.

In 1998, for example, 51 percent of voc-tech students failed the English Language Arts portion of the MCAS test, and 81 percent failed the math portion. Even the highest performing voc-tech schools in 1998 were classified as "Low Performing" when measured by the early MCAS proficiency index.

Few doubted the abilities of voc-tech students; rather, they objected to what was widely seen at the time as a mismatch between testing and curriculum.

"The results make it seem like voc-ed students are slow, but that is not at all the case," one graduate of Blue Hills Regional Technical School in Canton declared in 2000. "MCAS results generalize, rather than looking at the unique education that exists in a vocational school."

The concern shared by many was that the effort to meet higher academic standards, including MCAS, would force voc-tech schools to shift time away from the vocational side of their curriculum, thus undermining their core educational model.

The Massachusetts Association of Vocational Administrators (MAVA) filed legislation in 2001 to recognize the unique aspects of voc-tech education. Under their proposal, the attainment of a high school diploma would be based on a high-stakes test for both vocational skill competency and integrated academic proficiency. Voc-tech students would not be excluded from MCAS.

Nearly half the Legislature supported the proposal; however, state leaders took a wait-and-see position.

Opposition Becomes Enthusiasm—and Success

Within a few years, the voc-tech community dropped any remaining opposition to the new, more stringent academic standards.

One reason the voc-tech community's ongoing commitment to the integration of academic and vocational skills, both on their campuses and in their communities.

Throughout the late 1990s, voc-tech schools redoubled their efforts to smooth the transitions of their graduates from secondary to postsecondary education; they further strengthened already dynamic links to the business community; and they worked to align their general academic program more closely with the burgeoning postsecondary opportunities available to their graduates in an increasingly technological economy.

The statistics tell the story:

- Between 2001 and 2007, the Average Performance Index (API) for regional voc-tech and county agricultural schools went from 53.2 to 82.4, the greatest increase of any subgroup.

- By 2008, 96 percent of voc-tech students were passing both the English and Math MCAS tests — better than the 94 percent average for all students in the state — with many schools posting 100 percent passing rates.

Succeeding Under Ed Reform

Average Performance Index (API)
Regional voc-tech and county agricultural schools

2001: 53.2 **+55%** 2007: 82.4

Source: *Massachusetts Department of Elementary and Secondary Education*

Practicality and Hard Work Prove Their Worth

Looking back at the post-1993 era, it is easy to cite various factors for the voc-tech community's academic renaissance. But the simplest answer may be that voc-tech continued to succeed by adhering to its tradition of practicality and hard work.

According to research from High Schools That Work, an organization with over 1,100 member schools nationwide, the most successful voc-tech schools are those that most fully integrate college-preparatory academics with vocational courses.

Some might have predicted that the Commonwealth's unique voc-tech model — in which students alternate weekly between academics and their technical specialty — would have buckled under the strain of increased academic requirements.

It turned out that voc-tech students, with only half the academic time as their peers in comprehensive high schools, succeeded precisely because their academic studies were *reinforced* by the time devoted to ever-more sophisticated technical aspects of their education.

VI. The Challenges Facing 'Third-Generation' Voc-Tech Schools

The list of successes that flowed from the MERA is long, but few are more impressive than the ongoing success of the Commonwealth's voc-tech high schools. Over the nearly 30 years since education reform, these schools have transformed themselves.

Upon a solid and traditional foundation of vocational and technical excellence, these schools have built an increasingly impressive record of academic achievement.

The more than 50,000 students currently enrolled in these third-generation voc-tech schools — and the many who will follow them — have every reason to expect they will enjoy both the academic preparation and vocational training required of the highly skilled workforce of the twenty-first century.

But if those expectations are to be fulfilled, ongoing challenges must be met, both within the schools themselves and among the ranks of leaders in their districts. They include:

- Manage academic and vocational curriculum integration and alignment
- Provide student support services and professional development
- Meet high standards of evaluation and accountability
- Insure institutional fiscal stability
- Maintain strong industry-business ties to insure currency

Doing so will required a dual strategy centered on identity and autonomy.

Identity

On the one hand, the voc-tech community must defend its identity—exemplified in the practice of alternating weeks of vocational and instruction—and the autonomy of local governance that stands apart from that of other public schools.

Maintaining a firm identity for voc-tech schools requires constantly educating the families of potential students about the opportunities in their communities, building awareness of the career value that a voc-tech education represents, and fighting for necessary funding.

Much like charter public schools and the state's network of Catholic and parochial schools, Massachusetts's voc-tech high schools are schools of choice. They are not for everyone. But they occupy a vital place in the state's educational mosaic.

Vocational educators and administrators know from long experience that students who choose a voc-tech education, particularly in a regional district, are not settling for something less than what may be available to them in their hometown. They are making an active choice to become a member of a distinct community that puts them on course for a rigorous, comprehensive, and career-oriented education.

Autonomy

The Commonwealth's 26 regional vocational-technical schools (including two county agricultural schools) have been particularly successful. One of the reasons is that each school acts as its own school district, giving it the autonomy to address student needs that are distinct from those of traditional high school students.

In general, granting additional autonomy to certain schools or types of schools is not something that comes naturally to school districts, and educational policy makers should protect this important ingredient in vocational schools' success.

Voc-tech education must be able to discern and choose what is truly innovative and useful in an educational landscape that is often characterized by political pressures and instructional fads.

That freedom, combined with the tireless efforts of countless individuals over more than a century, has enabled the state's industrial, trade, and voc-tech schools to produce generations of well-trained and educated workers who have helped make Massachusetts one of the nation's economic leaders.

In recent years, however, the level of state commitment to this distinctive brand of education — along with regulatory changes — has raised concerns through the voc-tech education community.

Simply put, a strong and ongoing commitment from the state is essential. That commitment must include a recognition that voc-tech schools should continue to enjoy the autonomy they have long enjoyed.

Pioneer Institute Recommendations for Massachusetts Vocational-Technical Education

Our concluding recommendations are aimed at helping shape the thinking of policy makers to ensure that Massachusetts retains its status as the gold standard for voc-tech education for the nation.

Reverse recent changes that weaken voc-tech admissions policies

Since 1906, voc-tech schools have enjoyed a multifaceted admissions process that has helped make Massachusetts a national model for voc-tech education. The process was devised to ensure that a student's decision to apply would not be simply an alternative to the school in their home community, but a well-informed choice.

- Schools could consider the behavior and middle-school attendance records of applicants, important for students being trained in the safe use of sophisticated machinery.
- Admissions procedures for voc-tech schools didn't involve exams, writing samples, review of MCAS scores, or consideration of special education status.

- Optional interviews helped gauge applicants' interest and seriousness for what is, after all, a more expensive educational alternative.
- Middle school guidance counselors' recommendations could provide insight into an applicant's maturity, academic ability, and work ethic.
- Finally, individual school admissions policies had to be approved by the state.

Despite the proven record of success of this admissions procedure, the Commonwealth in 2021 took a step away from protecting voc-tech autonomy by adjusting their admissions processes. The likely effect of the following policy changes will be the admission of more students who are either a poor fit for the voc-tech environment or who are simply unprepared for the unique educational experience they are undertaking:

1. **Grade promotion and weakening of academic standards**
   Vocational schools and programs are now to condition admission on a student having been promoted to the grade required for admission to the school or program. Previously, in addition to grade promotion, students had been required to pass both English and mathematics.

2. **In most cases, a student's record of absences cannot be considered**
   Criteria for admission to a voc-tech school may not consider a student's record of excused absences during middle school. Previously, any absence from school could have been considered.

3. **'Minor' disciplinary infractions cannot be considered**
   Admissions criteria may not consider "a minor behavior or disciplinary infraction." Under the new rules, unless a student has been suspended from school for 10 days, it is considered a minor disciplinary infraction and cannot be considered. Previously, any suspension could be considered.

4. The state may impose a lottery system on voc-tech schools

According to the new regulations: *"Vocational schools and programs that use selective criteria shall not use criteria that have the effect of disproportionately excluding persons of a particular race, color, national origin, sex, gender identity, sexual orientation, religion, or disability unless they demonstrate that (1) such criteria have been validated as essential to participation in vocational programs; and (2) alternative equally valid criteria that do not have such a disproportionate adverse effect are unavailable. Selective criteria shall be approved annually by the school's board of trustees or school committee. The superintendent of the vocational school or program shall submit an annual attestation to the Department that the admissions policy of the school or program complies with federal and state law and any relevant guidelines issued by the Department or the U.S. Department of Education."*

State education officials may now take actions to address cases where they determine that voc-tech admissions policies are not in compliance with applicable state and federal laws and regulations. Such intervention may require an admissions lottery.

Previously, a lottery was one method for schools that did not want to use a selective admissions process. Prior to 2020–2021, voc-tech schools would send their admissions policies to DESE for approval. Now, the state provides technical assistance only, and does not approve individual policies. However, the state retains the power to require that schools institute an admissions lottery.

Summary: This recent replacement of voc-tech schools' longstanding admissions process with the potential threat of a lottery system chips away at the autonomy voc-tech schools have earned and that has been a key ingredient in their success. State policy makers should reverse the changes outlined above and restore full autonomy over admissions policies to voc-tech districts and schools.

Ensure Grade 8 students are aware of their voc-tech options

In order to ensure the broadest possible pool of qualified applicants, voc-tech schools must have unobstructed access to all eligible students. Only by providing complete information about the academic and vocational opportunities available to students currently completing Grade 8 can voc-tech schools ensure equal opportunity to all who have both the ability and interest to pursue admission.

The state Department of Elementary and Secondary Education (DESE) must commit itself to enforcing informational access to voc-tech materials for all students in Grade 8.

Recent regulatory changes have modified the selective admissions process that had existed largely unchanged since 1906, yet voc-tech schools continue to offer a distinctive alternative to students whose interests and aptitude make them a good fit.

Expand access to voc-tech education

Voc-tech education's long record of success should stand as sufficient grounds for expanding the number of available seats to accommodate the approximately 5,000 Massachusetts students who would like to attend such a school but must instead remain on a waiting list while they attend the regular high school in their community.

Even as K–12 enrollment in Massachusetts public schools declined in the early twenty-first century, the popularity of voc-tech schools increased — by 12.9 percent between 2004 and 2015. Seven years later, it remains as strong as ever, with approximately 5,000 students on voc-tech waiting lists.

Some students seek the vocational offerings available at their district high school, while others would prefer to attend a nearby regional voc-tech school to take advantage of the wider choice of equipment and offerings.

Just as importantly, there are 52 Massachusetts cities and towns in which students have no ready access to either district or regional voc-tech education. Of those, 32 are concentrated in Berkshire and Hampshire counties, highlighting a divide between urban/suburban and rural students.

Moreover, as noted repeatedly throughout this book, the percentage of low-income students attending and succeeding at voc-tech schools is above the statewide average. Further, the longest waiting lists are in districts that serve large numbers of students who come from low-income families, belong to a minority group, and/or speak English as a second language.

Voc-tech schools have long been a force for greater equality of opportunity in education, training, and job markets. Expansion would serve to meet the needs of all students.

While data show that voc-tech education is more expensive, a 2015 Pioneer Institute study found that accommodating another 5,000 students would require an increase of less than 0.5 percent of the state's K–12 education budget, or about $20 million (in 2015 dollars).[142]

Conduct a follow-up study of voc-tech graduates

The 1993 Massachusetts Education Reform Act changed the vocational quality of service standard from a "time on task" measure — which had been in effect since 1906 — to an "outcome based" standard.

In the nearly 30 years since the MERA was passed, there have been no longitudinal studies conducted to determine the impact of this significant change on voc-tech education.

In addition, the recent regulatory changes that modified the selective admissions process also mark a significant change whose impact needs to be determined.

We urge the DESE to hire an independent contractor to conduct a longitudinal, five-year, follow-up study of voc-tech graduates to determine the effects of these key changes to admission and evaluation processes.

Establish autonomous voc-tech representation within DESE

The DESE should establish a Division of Career/Vocational-Technical and Agricultural Education under the leadership of an Associate Commissioner. The Division of Occupational Education was eliminated by the MERA, although vocational education divisional status had been maintained since 1909 and proven its value over the years.

In the 2020–2021 school year, there were 54,300 students in rigorous and extensive voc-tech and agricultural programs throughout the state, and another 9,140 students in career technical courses.

Approximately 20 percent of Massachusetts's high school students participate in some form of career voc-tech education. They should have appropriate visibility and representation within the DESE.

■ ■ ■

Dr. Wilfrid J. Savoie spent 33 years in vocational-technical education as a teacher and administrator, including 16 years as superintendent-director of the Blue Hills Regional Technical School District. He previously had worked in the electronics industry and served in the U.S. Army. Dr. Savoie has been a consultant in many local, state, national, and international groups and programs regarding voc-tech education. He is a graduate of New Bedford Vocational High School, Wentworth Institute of Technology, Northeastern University, and Fitchburg State University. Dr. Savoie has been an outspoken advocate for vocational education for fifty years and is currently writing The History of Vocational Education in Massachusetts: A Model for the Nation.

Endnotes

1   Labor Market Information, Long-Term Occupational Projections, 2018–2028, Department of Unemployment Assistance, Economic Research Department, at https://lmi.dua.eol.mass.gov/.

2   The Commission on Industrial and Technical Education, Report, April 1906, Conclusions, 18–20, State House Library, Boston, Massachusetts.

3   See https://www.mbae.org/preparing-for-the-future-employer-perspectives-on-work-readiness-skills/.

4   See https://nces.ed.gov/fastfacts/display.asp?id=372

5   See https://www.brookings.edu/research/reconnecting-massachusetts-gateway-cities-lessons-learned-and-an-agenda-for-renewal/.

6   Data from Massachusetts DESE.

7   Fred M. Newmann, Robert A. Rutter, and Marshall S. Smith, "Organizational Factors that Affect School Sense of Efficacy, Community, and Expectations," *Sociology of Education*, Vol. 62 (1989), 224.

8   Quoted in "Technically Speaking—Demand Is Strong for Modern Vocational Education," Peter Schworm, *The Boston Globe*, May 13, 2007.

9   See https://www.doe.mass.edu/ccte/cvte/.

10 Mary H. Metz, "How social class differences shape teachers' work," in *Contexts of Teaching in Secondary School*, M.W. McLaughlin, ed. (New York: Teachers College Press, 1990), 40–107.

11 Schworm, ibid.

12 David Hawkins, "I, Thou, and It," in *The Informed Vision: Essays on Learning and Human Nature* (New York: Agathon Books), 58.

13 Philp Kaufman, Peter Teitelbaum, and Denise Bradby, "High Schools that Work and Whole School Reform: Raising Academic Achievement of Vocational Completers through the Reform of School Practice," (Berkeley, California: National Center for Research in Vocational Education, 2000).

14 John Seeley Brown, Allan Collins, and Paul Duguid, "Situated Cognition and the Culture of Learning," *Educational Researcher*, Vol. 18, No. 1 (1989).

15 Gene Bottoms and Deede Sharp, "Teaching for Understanding Through Integration of Academic and Technical Education" (Atlanta: Southern Regional Education Board, 1996), 58.

16 MASSMEP, "The New Worcester Vocational School: A Story of Persistence and Innovation," http://www.massmac.org/newsline/0605/article01.htm.

17 "Dropout Rates in Massachusetts Public Schools 2012–13," Massachusetts Department of Elementary and Secondary Education (DESE), see http://www.doe.mass.edu/infoservices/reports/dropout/2012-2013/.

18 James Brosnan, telephone interview, Sept. 10, 2014.

19 "Dropout Rates in Massachusetts Public Schools 2012–13," Massachusetts DESE.

20 U. S. Department of Education, Office of Vocational and Adult Education, see http://www.ed.gov/print/about/offices/list/ovae/index.html.

21 Greg Bialecki, Massachusetts Secretary of Housing and Economic Development, remarks delivered at Advanced Manufacturing Roundtable, held at Blackstone Valley Regional Vocational Technical High School, Sept. 8, 2014.

22 Stefan Czaporowski, telephone interview, Sept. 4, 2014.

23 Brosnan, interview.

24 Chris Chapman, "Trends in High School Dropout and Completion Rates in the United States: 1972–2009," October 2011, National Center for Education Statistics, U.S. Department of Education, Introduction, 1.

25 Robert Balfanz, "Building a Grad Nation: Progress and Challenge in Ending the High School Dropout Epidemic," Annual Update 2012, Everyone Graduates Center at Johns Hopkins University, Executive Summary, 1.

26 Annual Dropout Rates by School Type, Massachusetts Department of Elementary & Secondary Education (DESE).

27 Ibid.

28 David Ferreira, interview, Massachusetts Association of Vocational Administrators, May 8, 2012.

29 Wilfrid J. Savoie, excerpts from "The History of Vocational Education in Massachusetts," unpublished manuscript, July 14, 2008, citing The Commission on Industrial and Technical Education, Report, April 1906, State House Library, Boston, Massachusetts.

30 James Kulik, *Curriculum Tracks and High School Vocational Studies* (Ann Arbor: University of Michigan, 1998).

31 Stephen Plank, Stephanie DeLuca, and Angela Estacion, *Dropping Out of High School and the Place of Career and Technical Education* (St. Paul: National Research Center for Career and Technical Education, University of Minnesota, 2005).

32 "Career and Technical Education's Role in Dropout Prevention and Recovery," Association for Career and Technical Education, June 2007, 3.

33 Ibid.

34 Sheila Harrity, interview, April 2, 2012.

35 Massachusetts Alliance for Business Education report, "Preparing for the Future: Employer Perspectives on Work Readiness Skills," Boston, 2006. See https://www.mbae.org/preparing-for-the-future-employer-perspectives-on-work-readiness-skills/

36 Charles Lyons, interview, March 16, 2012.

37 See DESE, http://www.doe.mass.edu/infoservices/reports/gradrates/dropoutvsgrad.html.

38 See DESE, http://www.doe.mass.edu/infoservices/data/sims/.

39 Ferreira, interview.

40 Anthony Steele II, then Director of Curriculum and Student Support Services, Blackstone Valley Regional Vocational Technical High School, interview, May 18, 2012.

41 Dr. Judith Klimkiewicz, then superintendent of Nashoba Valley Technical School, interview, March 21, 2012.

42 Lyons, interview.

43 See DESE, dropout rates, available at http://www.doe.mass.edu/infoservices/reports/dropout/

44 Harrity, interview.

45   Symonds, Bottoms, and Fitzpatrick, "Promise and Potential: Madison Park Technical Vocational High School, the BPS Acceleration Agenda and a Pathway of Opportunity for Boston Students," Boston Public Schools, Office of Career and Technical Education (Boston, 2012).

46   Alison L. Fraser and William Donovan, "Hands-On Achievement: Why Massachusetts Vocational Technical Schools Have Low Dropout Rates," (Boston: Pioneer Institute, white paper No. 93, January 2013).

47   "Catholic Schools: Communities of Academic Excellence," NCEA Parent News, National Catholic Education Association, July 2016.

48   Heather Gossart, telephone interview, April 7, 2017.

49   Kathy Mears, telephone interview, May 2, 2017.

50   Office of Career/Vocational Technical Education, Massachusetts Department of Elementary & Secondary Education (DESE). See https://www.doe.mass.edu/ccte/cvte/.

51   David Ferreira, telephone interview, Feb. 10, 2017.

52   Press release, Office of Gov. Charlie Baker, Jan. 22, 2016.

53   Press release, Office of Gov. Charlie Baker, March 3, 2017.

54   Catherine Tumber, Barry Bluestone, et al., "The Critical Importance of Vocational and Technical Education in the Commonwealth," Northeastern University School of Public Policy & Urban Affairs, January 2016.

55   Ibid, Key Findings, 6.

56   "Massachusetts Chapter 74 Career/Vocational Technical Education Program Directory," 6–12, Massachusetts DESE, January 2016.

57   Labor and Workforce Development, Massachusetts Executive Office of Labor and Workforce Development, http://www.mass.gov/lwd/economic-data/.

58   Ernest Houle, interview, March 8, 2017.

59   John Lafleche, interview, March 21, 2017.

60   Edward Bouquillon, interview, March 7, 2017.

61   Ferreira, interview.

62   James Vaznis, "As applications drop, BC High School ponders its future," The Boston Globe, May 6, 2017.

63 "The State of Catholic Schools in the US," *The Catholic World Report*, May 31, 2011.

64 Ibid.

65 Mears, interview.

66 Victoria Kelly, telephone interview, April 10, 2017.

67 "Graduate Statistics," Mercy Career & Technical High School web site, see latest figures at https://www.mercycte.org/about/graduate-statistics.

68 "Forging Futures with Faith and Focus," Mercy Career & Technical High School 2016 Annual Report. See https://www.mercycte.org/giving/annual-report.

69 Ibid.

70 Max Larkin, "What the State Sees Inside Boston Public Schools: Change, 'Bright Spots,' and Lots of Dysfunction," March 18, 2020, https://www.wbur.org/edify/2020/03/18/bps-report-highlights.

71 Martin Finucane and Jacqueline Tempera, "Review ordered at Boston's Madison Park High School," *The Boston Globe*, March 14, 2014.

72 Kevin McCaskill, telephone interview, July 16, 2020.

73 Brian Jacob, "What we know about Career and Technical Education in High School," Brookings Institution, Oct. 5, 2017, see www.brookings.edu/research/what-we-know-about-career-and-technical-education-in-high-school/.

74 Shaun M. Dougherty, Shaun M., "The Effect of Career and Technical Education on Human Capital Accumulation: Causal Evidence from Massachusetts," University of Connecticut, Center for Education Policy Analysis, Spring 2018, see https://direct.mit.edu/edfp/article/13/2/119/10291/The-Effect-of-Career-and-Technical-Education-on.

75 Madison Park Technical Vocational High School, Draft Turnaround Plan Component of School Redesign Grant Application, Massachusetts DESE, Executive Summary, May 26, 2016, 2.

76 Ibid, ix.

77 Ibid.

78 James Vaznis, "Madison Park headmaster wasn't certified," *The Boston Globe*, Sept. 13, 2014.

79 James Vaznis, "A call to fix or shut Madison Park school," *The Boston Globe*, July 14, 2014.

80 James Vaznis, "After protest, most Madison Park students get schedules," *The Boston Globe*, September 9, 2014.

81 New England Association of Schools and Colleges, Inc., Visiting Team Report, Madison Park Technical Vocational High School, Oct. 25, 2018, 95.

82 "DESE and BPS Agree to a New Model for Improvement in District," at Boston Public Schools website, see https://www. bostonpublicschools.org/site/default.aspx?PageType=3&Domain ID=4&ModuleInstanceID=14&ViewID=6446EE88-D30C-497E-9316-3F8874B3E108&RenderLoc=0&FlexDataID=27958&Page ID=0.

83 Ibid, 2.

84 See https://www.doe.mass.edu/turnaround/howitworks/ monitoring.html.

85 Madison Park Technical Vocational High School draft turnaround plan, component of School Redesign Grant application (MP draft plan), May 2016, 4.

86 Ibid, 6.

87 New England Association of Schools and Colleges, Inc., Visiting Team Report, Madison Park Technical Vocational High School (NEASC report), Oct. 25, 2018, 84.

88 MP draft plan, 3.

89 MP draft plan, 48–49.

90 NEASC report, 59.

91 Data provided by Madison Park Technical Vocational High School.

92 NEASC report, 200.

93 MP draft plan, 36.

94 MP draft plan, 90.

95 School and District Profiles, Massachusetts Department of Elementary and Secondary Education, see https://profiles.doe. mass.edu/general/general.aspx?topNavID=1&leftNavId=100& orgcode=03480605&orgtypecode=6.

96   Sheila Harrity, telephone interview, Dec. 20, 2021.

97   Massachusetts Department of Elementary and Secondary Education (DESE).

98   "The Long, Hard, Litigious, Heartbreaking, Triumphant Struggle to Build a New Voke School," *Worcester Magazine*, Feb. 13, 2003.

99   Ibid.

100 "It's All Academic," Worcester Technical High School, supplement to the *Worcester Business Journal* and *Worcester Magazine*, 2006, 8.

101 Harrity, interview.

102 "Sheila Harrity, 2014 MetLife/NASSP High School Principal of the Year," National Blue Ribbon Schools Program website, see https://nationalblueribbonschools.ed.gov/2013/10/nbrs-principal-named-national-high-school-principal-of-the-year/.

103 "Building on a Dream," Worcester Technical High School, supplement to the *Worcester Business Journal and Worcester Magazine*, 2006, 3.

104 "Breakthrough Schools," National Association of Secondary School Principals, see https://www.nassp.org/breakthrough-schools/.

105 Harrity became superintendent of Montachusett Regional Vocational Technical School in Fitchburg in 2014.

106 National Blue Ribbon Schools Program, U.S. Department of Education, https://www2.ed.gov/programs/nclbbrs/index.html.

107 National Blue Ribbon Schools Program, see https://nationalblueribbonschools.ed.gov/awardwinners/winning/13ma002pu_worcester_technical_high_school.html.

108 George Johnson, telephone interview, Dec. 16, 2021.

109 See https://www.putnamvta.com/shop-programs.

110 Kevin McCaskill, telephone interview, Dec. 28, 2021.

111 Graduation Rate Report (District) for All Students 4-Year Graduation Rate, School and District Profiles, DESE, see https://profiles.doe.mass.edu/statereport/gradrates.aspx.

112 Roger L. Putnam Vocational Technical Academy, School and District Profiles, DESE, see https://profiles.doe.mass.edu/profiles/student.aspx?orgcode=02810620&orgtypecode=6&&fycode=2009.

113 "Editorial: Financial audit shows Putnam Vocational High School failed Springfield students," *Springfield Republican*, March 29, 2011.

114 Gilbert Traverso, telephone interview, Dec. 21, 2021.

115 Change Agent, A Dynamic Principal Has Given New Meaning to the Phrase 'Putnam Pride,'" *BusinessWest*, March 11, 2014.

116 Ibid.

117 Ibid.

118 Johnson, interview.

119 Information Services, DESE, see https://www.doe.mass.edu/infoservices/reports/dropout/.

120 Lee-Clark, Bruce, "Decennial Report, Putnam Vocational Technical Academy, New England Association of Schools and Colleges Commission on Technical and Career Institutions, December 2014, 70.

121 Ibid, 73.

122 See www.causeiq.com/organizations/roger-l-putnam-technical-fund,263769868/.

123 See Alison L. Fraser, "Vocational Technical Education in Massachusetts," (Pioneer Institute, white paper No. 42, October 2008).

124 Alison L. Fraser and William Donovan, "Hands-On Achievement: Why Massachusetts Vocational Technical Schools Have Low Dropout Rates," (Pioneer Institute, white paper No. 72, January 2013).

125 Massachusetts Department of Elementary and Secondary Education (DESE), "Charter School Fact Sheet, Directory, and Application History." See www.doe.mass.edu/charter/about.html.

126 Ken Ardon, "Enrollment Trends in Massachusetts," Pioneer Institute, September 2008, and Ken Ardon, "Enrollment Trends in Massachusetts: An Update," Pioneer Institute, October 2012. Since the updated 2012 report, enrollment has remained relatively flat.

127 See https://www.doe.mass.edu/finance/statistics/. DESE spending figures do not include acquisition of fixed assets or debt service costs.

128 See http://www.massschoolbuildings.org/building/funding/reimbursements.

129 Data from "2010 Needs Survey Report," Massachusetts School Building Authority, 2011.

130 For a history of regionalization, see "School District Consolidation in Massachusetts" at http://www.doe.mass.edu/finance/regional/.

131 The Commission on Industrial and Technical Education, Report, April 1906, 18; Wright & Potter Printing Co., State Printers, 18 Post Office Square 1906, Published by Teachers College, Columbia University, New York.

132 Ibid., 19.

133 Ibid., 19.

134 Massachusetts Acts and Resolves, Chapter 505 of the Acts of 1906; Massachusetts Acts and Resolves, Massachusetts Chapter 457, Acts of 1909, 459; Wilfrid J. Savoie, material from *The History of Vocational Education in Massachusetts: A Model for the Nation,* unpublished manuscript; Annual Report of the Department of Education, Massachusetts, Year Ending June 30, 1961, Part I, 519.

135 Savoie, *The History of Vocational Education in Massachusetts: A Model for the Nation.*

136 National Defense Act of 1958, see https://history.house.gov/HouseRecord/Detail/15032436195.

137 Vocational Education Act of 1963, see text https://www.govinfo.gov/content/pkg/STATUTE-77/pdf/STATUTE-77-Pg403.pdf#page=13 and analysis https://files.eric.ed.gov/fulltext/ED119027.pdf.

138 Franklin P. Rice, editor, *The Worcester of Eighteen Hundred and Ninety-Eight. Fifty Years a City.,* 123–131. (Worcester, Massachusetts: F.S. Blanchard & Company, 1899).

139 Ibid, 189.

140 Savoie, *The History of Vocational Education in Massachusetts: A Model for the Nation.*

141 See www.mbae.org/preparing-for-the-future-employer-perspectives-on-work-readiness-skills/.

142 See Ken Ardon and Alison L. Fraser, "Expanding Access to Vocational-Technical Education in Massachusetts" (Boston: Pioneer Institute, white paper No. 136, October 2015).